Managing Innovation and Entrepreneurship

D1579345

Managing Innovation and Entrepreneurship

ROBERT D. HISRICH

Thunderbird School of Global Management

CLAUDINE KEARNEY

University College Dublin

Los Angeles | London | New Delhi
Singapore | Washington DC

Los Angeles | London | New Delhi
Singapore | Washington DC

FOR INFORMATION:

SAGE Publications, Inc.
2455 Teller Road
Thousand Oaks, California 91320
E-mail: order@sagepub.com

SAGE Publications Ltd.
1 Oliver's Yard
55 City Road
London EC1Y 1SP
United Kingdom

SAGE Publications India Pvt. Ltd.
B 1/I 1 Mohan Cooperative Industrial Area
Mathura Road, New Delhi 110 044
India

SAGE Publications Asia-Pacific Pte. Ltd.
3 Church Street
#10-04 Samsung Hub
Singapore 049483

Acquisitions Editor: Patricia Quinlin
Associate Editor: Maggie Stanley
Editorial Assistant: Katie Guarino
Production Editor: Laura Barrett
Copy Editor: Megan Markanich
Typesetter: C&M Digitals (P) Ltd.
Proofreader: Stefanie Storholt
Indexer: Michael Ferreira
Cover Designer: Anupama Krishan
Marketing Manager: Liz Thornton
Permissions Editor: Jennifer Barron

Printed in the United States of America

Library of Congress Cataloging-in-Publication Data

Hisrich, Robert D.

Managing innovation and entrepreneurship / Robert D. Hisrich, Thunderbird School of Global Management Claudine Kearney, University College Dublin.

pages cm

Includes bibliographical references and index.

ISBN 978-1-4522-4135-7 (pbk. : alk. paper)

1. Entrepreneurship. 2. Technological innovations—Management. 3. Entrepreneurship—Case studies. 4. Technological innovations—Management—Case studies. I. Kearney, Claudine. II. Title.

HB615.H5763 2014
658.4'21—dc23   2013012632

This book is printed on acid-free paper.

Certified Chain of Custody
Promoting Sustainable Forestry
www.sfiprogram.org
SFI-01268

SUSTAINABLE FORESTRY INITIATIVE

SFI label applies to text stock

13 14 15 16 10 9 8 7 6 5 4 3 2 1

Brief Contents

Detailed Contents

Preface

Innovation and entrepreneurship are important to individuals, organizations, and governments and significantly impact the economic development of both developed and developing economies. The two are not just a part of new ventures but exist as well in organizations in the private, public, and social sectors. Innovation occurs both inside and outside organizations and is becoming increasingly critical to success due to the impact of globalization, rapidly changing technology, shorter life cycles, and hypercompetition. Innovation includes the creation of new combinations, new ways of doing things, new methods of production, new channels of distribution and distribution methods, new products and services, and the formation of new ventures both inside and outside organizations.

To better understand these concepts of innovation and entrepreneurship both inside and outside the organization, this book is composed of 10 chapters divided into four sections. Section 1, Discovering the Origins of Innovation and Entrepreneurship, consists of Chapters 1 through 3 and discusses the origins of innovation and entrepreneurship as well as the core benefits to the organization particularly in enhancing its performance. An organization needs to allow individuals and groups to identify, select, evaluate, and operationalize innovative activities that address potential opportunities. The section concludes with a discussion of the concepts of creativity, the creative process, the types of innovation, the innovation process, and sources of innovation and entrepreneurship.

Section 2, Managing Innovation and Entrepreneurship, consists of Chapters 4 through 6 and presents ideas on the management of innovation and entrepreneurship. Developing an innovative culture, organizational structure, and a management system and orientation are fundamental in developing and growing an innovative, entrepreneurial organization. Following a discussion of establishing a system for assessing, monitoring, and evaluating the internal innovation process as well as the external environment, the section concludes with a discussion of the aspects, role, and use of design thinking and how it takes place and benefits several organizations.

Section 3, Operationalizing Innovation and Entrepreneurship, consists of Chapters 7 and 8 and deals with operationalizing innovation and entrepreneurship in an organization. The focus is on building and planning the innovation case and establishing a process for developing innovation, such as the product planning and development process, as well as accessing the risks involved.

Section 4, Making It All Happen: The Future of Innovation and Entrepreneurship, consists of Chapters 9 and 10 and focuses on both domestic and international innovation and entrepreneurship and their similarities and differences. Financial and nonfinancial performance measures are discussed. This section and the book conclude by presenting the impact of innovation and entrepreneurship on consumers, organizations, governments, and society now and in the future.

Robert D. Hisrich

Claudine Kearney

Acknowledgments

Many individuals from all over the world—corporate executives, entrepreneurs, government officials, inventors, and managers in both the profit and not for profit sectors and professors—have made this book possible. Our thanks go to the following reviewers for their thoughtful comments and suggestions at various stages of this manuscript: Nader Asgary, Bentley University; Dr. Robin Oxer Berenson, Franklin University; Pelin Bicen, PhD, at Penn State University-Erie; J. Palmer Brown, University of Alabama; William G. Donohoo, California State University San Bernardino; Azita Hirsa, The Sage Colleges; Chung-Shing Lee, Pacific Lutheran University; Judith J. Lee, DBA, Golden Gate University; Kenneth J. McLeod, PhD, Department of Bioengineering, Watson School of Engineering, Binghamton University; Klara Nelson, The University of Tampa; Dr. Joseph C. Picken. The Institute for Innovation & Entrepreneurship at The University of Texas at Dallas; Dr. Robert D. Russell, School of Business Administration, Penn State Harrisburg; Dr. Rajiv R. Shah, School of Management, The University of Texas at Dallas; Verinder Syal, CEO, Syal Consult, Northwestern University; and Fred J. Ziolkowski, Purdue University. Our special thanks go to two members of the editorial team at SAGE—Patricia Quinlin and Katie Guarino—for their assistance, prodding, and support. Special thanks go to our research assistants—Tracy Droessler and Fabienne Jolivert—for their dedicated researching, editing, and writing. And our utmost appreciation goes to Carol Pacelli for her research and editing and without whom this book would never have been prepared in a timely manner.

We are deeply indebted to Tina Hisrich; Kary and Katy Hisrich; Kelly, Rich, Rachel, Andrew, and Sarah Nash; Kaiya; and Patricia and Syl Kearney for their support and their understanding of the time needed to develop and write this book. It is to them and the spirit of innovation and entrepreneurship that this book is specifically dedicated.

DISCOVERING THE ORIGINS OF INNOVATION AND ENTREPRENEURSHIP

CHAPTER 1

The Entrepreneurial/ Innovative Economy

W hat is meant by the term *entrepreneurship?* What is innovation, and why is it important? What is the link between entrepreneurship and innovation? How does entrepreneurship and innovation improve organizational performance? What is the contribution of entrepreneurship and innovation to an economy?

Scenario: Facebook

Mark Zuckerberg is the CEO and cofounder of Facebook. He was born on May 14th, 1984, in New York. Zuckerberg is a computer programmer and Internet entrepreneur. In February 2004 from a dorm room at Harvard College, he cofounded Facebook with roommates and fellow students Eduardo Saverin, Dustin Moskovitz, and Chris Hughes. Initially, Facebook limited membership to students at Harvard, but later this expanded to other universities such as MIT, Yale, Princeton, and Stanford. Membership became available to students at other universities then to high school students. In September 2006, membership was open to anyone ages 13 and over with an e-mail address, resulting in 50,000 new users a day joining Facebook.

Zuckerberg dropped out of Harvard after his sophomore year, moving Facebook to Palo Alto, California. Since Facebook was growing rapidly, Zuckerberg needed investment money, so he made contact with Silicon Valley venture capitalists, receiving his first investment of $500,000. By the end of 2004, Facebook had reached 1 million users; it reached 5 million users in 2005. In May 2005, Facebook received a major investment of $12.7 million from a venture capital firm, Accel Partners. In April 2006, Facebook raised $27.5 million from Greylock Partners, Meritech Capital Partners, and others. Soon, other companies wanted to buy the entire business. In 2006, Zuckerberg refused a $1 billion offer from Yahoo. In 2007, Microsoft offered $15 billion, and once again Zuckerberg refused.

Zuckerberg's core focus was on developing the site, opening the project to external developers, and adding additional features. Investors bought into Facebook without too much concern about how the company was going to make a profit. In October 2007, Facebook and Microsoft developed an advertising arrangement to cover international markets with Microsoft taking a $240 million equity stake in the company. By 2008, with over 100 million users, it was time to think about developing a profitable business model. To achieve this, Zuckerberg hired one of Google's star executives Sheryl Sandberg (as chief operating officer). She knew exactly how to build a company from the start-up phase to development. As Facebook grew, Zuckerberg continued to use the same energy and flexibility of a start-up with an unofficial motto of "Move Fast and Break Things." He was still closely involved in the details. Everyone at Facebook was expected to move fast with new programmers having a chance to write computer code that contributed to the site within their first days of employment.

Zuckerberg is recognized as a new type of entrepreneur. Since its formation in 2004, Facebook has found its way into the personal lives of 800 million people. Once in a while a breakthrough innovation and/or a business comes along that transforms an era by doing something very new and very big. Zuckerberg did this and turned social needs into a multibillion-dollar business. Facebook has changed the way hundreds of millions of people communicate and talk to each other. It has created not just a business but an entirely new culture.

In 2010, *Time* magazine named Zuckerberg their "Person of the Year"; *Vanity Fair* placed him at the top of their New Establishment list; and *Forbes* ranked him at No. 35—surpassing the late Steve Jobs, former Apple CEO, on their Forbes 400 list. In 2011, his personal wealth was estimated to be $17.5 billion. Facebook has astronomically grown to 901 million active users as of April 2012. More people have signed up on Facebook than live in the United States and European Union combined, with 30 million registered users in Britain alone.

Facebook's mission is to make the world more open and connected.

Zuckerberg practices what he preaches, sharing a lot about his personal life on his Facebook page, which is open for anyone to view. There have been questions about how people communicate on Facebook, about their privacy, and the sharing of information. Facebook asserts that it gives users full control over their privacy and what they choose to communicate. Zuckerberg believes that privacy is fundamental, but the big cultural change is that now more and more people are finding that they can build a reputation, disseminate interesting information, and be part of a new discovery process.

Facebook is not just a website; it is a platform. Software developers can write programs—apps—that then run on Facebook. These apps create a technology ecosystem with Facebook at the core. There are over 1 million different developers who have built things on Facebook. The question facing Facebook is this: How can they build all the things they want to? According to Zuckerberg, the answer was simply to build an ecosystem and make sure any developer from a student in a dorm to a small or large company can build things on the platform.

When Zuckerberg opened Facebook to developers, the biggest success was games. London is home to the second largest social gaming company. Kristian Sergerstrale, cofounder of Playfish, employs 350 people to make games for his 100 million regular players. Facebook has created an infrastructure for these and other games and social interactions. It is as much about that social interaction as it is about what is happening on the screen. This generates new revenue for Facebook, because game players pay money for virtual goods. They pay by sending money to Facebook to buy credits.

The creation of Facebook has led to lawsuits and accusations of privacy invasion; it has even inspired a Hollywood movie. The first legal dispute was filed in 2004 when Harvard students Cameron Winklevoss, Tyler Winklevoss, Divya Narendra, and others accused Zuckerberg of misleading them into thinking he would contribute to them developing a social network called HarvardConnection.com (which was later called ConnectU), while he was taking their ideas to develop a competitive product. The three issued a complaint to the *Harvard Crimson*, and an investigation was undertaken by the newspaper. The legal dispute resulted in an initial settlement of $65 million; however, the legal dispute over the issue proceeded into 2011 after Narendra and the Winklevosses claimed they were misguided about their stock value. Zuckerberg encountered another challenge in 2009 when the book *The Accidental Billionaires*, written by Ben Mezrich, was published. Mezrich was criticized for invented scenes, reimagined dialogue, and fictional characters of Zuckerberg's story. Mezrich sold the rights to screenwriter Aaron Sorkin, and the film *The Social Network* received eight Academy Award nominations. Zuckerberg had strong objection to the film's narrative and informed a reporter at *The*

New Yorker that numerous details in the film were incorrect. In spite of these obstacles and challenges, Zuckerberg's dorm project has come a long way since 2004, not just as a piece of technology but as a change in the way many people relate to each other. Facebook is a massive online social world that runs parallel with the real world. Many users spend more time online with their Facebook friends than meeting their real friends. A lot of people who would have otherwise lost contact stay in touch through Facebook. The next step for Facebook, according to Zuckerberg, is to allow people to connect to anything they want in any way they want.

On Friday, May 18, 2012, Facebook went public, pricing its initial public offering (IPO) at $38 per share. Facebook shares rose 0.6% to $38.23 at the close of business on its first day of trading. Approximately 570 million shares were traded and 70 million just at the IPO. Zuckerberg retains 533 million shares and voting control over Facebook. Zuckerberg's net worth increased by $100 million to $19.4 billion; he is now 26th on the Bloomberg Billionaires Index. The company's valuation at that time was more than Amazon.com, Kraft, Walt Disney, Cisco, and McDonald's. Facebook is the biggest technology business to go public since Google. The company had net income of $205 million in the first three months of 2012 on revenue of $1.06 billion. However, reflecting back, the stock has lost half its value since its IPO. Through hard work and commitment, Zuckerberg is now focusing on how well Facebook can do in the next 3 to 5 years with mobile as a path to generate revenue for the company. Facebook is a very controversial company. Zuckerberg has recognized his mistakes, stating that his biggest mistake was betting too much on HTML5, rather than focusing on native applications. Just as a culture of innovation and entrepreneurship is fundamental, so is the ability to learn from mistakes. Rather than being inhibited by their mistakes, Facebook has created an environment where they are very self-critical, and failure is both tolerated and learned from.

Introduction

As indicated in the scenario of Facebook, entrepreneurship and innovation do not just happen. It can be and in many cases is a risky and expensive investment to start a business and requires continuous investment and commitment in light of all the challenges and obstacles. This risk and expenses continue as established corporations continue to develop and implement entrepreneurial activity and innovation. Facebook's success indicates that it understood the importance of innovation, and even though it dealt with many challenges along the way, it has showed commitment, perseverance, and passion for pursuing entrepreneurial activity and innovation. To manage environmental complexity and uncertainty, firms become more entrepreneurial in order to identify and exploit new opportunities. Regardless of the economic climate, entrepreneurship and innovation is a dynamic process involving opportunities, individuals, organizations, risks, and resources.

Entrepreneurship and innovation is a topic of interest and research that has been developed over decades. Entrepreneurship is developing something new with value by dedicating the required time, commitment, and perseverance, undertaking the associated risks and rewards with the objective of achieving prosperity and wealth. This can be a new start-up organization or part of revitalizing an existing organization in response to an observed opportunity. The term *entrepreneurship* has traditionally been associated with starting a new business; however, more recently the term has been developed to incorporate social and political forms of entrepreneurial activity. Entrepreneurship is not only evident by new firms coming into the market but also by innovative and similar entries of existing firms into new markets. Entrepreneurship within a large organization it is referred to as *intrapreneurship* or *corporate entrepreneurship* (CE). Entrepreneurial activities vary significantly in relation to the type of organization and the level of creativity and innovation within the organization. Innovativeness is the first dimension that characterizes an entrepreneurial organization. Innovation creates more efficient and effective products, systems, services, technologies, or ideas that are accepted by markets, governments, and society.

This chapter provides the historic development of the core concepts of the evolution of entrepreneurship, historic development of key definitions of entrepreneurs, entrepreneurship and innovation as well as the link between them. Following this, there is a discussion on understanding an entrepreneurial and innovative economy—along with the core benefits of entrepreneurship and innovation to an economy. Entrepreneurship and innovation represent a unifying framework for successful management practice that can be attained by combining the key roles of managers and entrepreneurs. The chapter concludes by providing an overall framework of entrepreneurship and innovation that will serve as the foundation for the structure of this book.

Entrepreneurship—What It Means and Why It Is Important

There is no universally accepted definition of entrepreneurship; rather, entrepreneurship is a phenomenon with many components. It takes many forms such as private sector entrepreneurship, CE, public sector entrepreneurship (*governpreneurship*), and social entrepreneurship.

The Historic Development of Entrepreneurship

One of the first to be looked at as an entrepreneur was Marco Polo, who tried to set up trade routes to the Far East (Hisrich, Peters, and Shepherd, 2012). In the Middle Ages, the term *entrepreneur* was associated with an actor and an individual who managed large production projects—for example, an individual who manages architectural works such as castles, public buildings, or cathedrals. In major projects, the individual did not take risk but rather he/she managed the project utilizing the resources that the government usually provided. In the 17th century, an entrepreneur was an individual who entered into a contractual arrangement with the government to carry out a service or provide acquired products—for example, John Law, a Frenchman, was allowed to establish a royal bank. One of the earliest definitions of entrepreneurship was that of Richard Cantillion (1755), an economist, who described the entrepreneur as a rational decision maker who assumed the risk and provided management for the firm. He was the first to acknowledge that there is an entrepreneurial function within the economic system. In the 18th century, the entrepreneur was differentiated from what is today known as the venture capitalist. This differentiation was made because of industrialization. In the late 19th and early 20th centuries, entrepreneurship began to develop theoretically. In the 20th century, Joseph Schumpeter, an economist, made a significant contribution to the theoretical development of entrepreneurship. At that time, entrepreneurs were mostly viewed from an economic perspective. In the middle of the 20th century, the idea that entrepreneurs were innovators was established. Since then, innovation and newness is a fundamental aspect of entrepreneurship.

Historically, the term *entrepreneurship* has referred to an individual who takes on the risk of turning their vision into a successful business enterprise. Some definitions focus on entrepreneurship as the creation of new organizations, while others focus on wealth creation and ownership. This recognizes other forms of ownership—for example, franchising, corporate venturing, management takeover, and family business. Some have adopted the opportunity-based view and suggested that entrepreneurship is about the discovery and exploitation of profitable market opportunities.

Over the past four decades, entrepreneurship has extended beyond individual's efforts to follow their vision to include entrepreneurship within existing corporations. This has been referred to as CE as well as previously intra-corporate entrepreneurship, corporate venturing, organizational entrepreneurship, innovation, and intrapreneurship. Corporate entrepreneurship is a process whereby individuals within an organization undertake innovative opportunities outside their current role. Companies like IBM recognized the value of CE in increasing corporate growth; 3M and Google has been known for decades as an entrepreneurial company with a strong corporate culture that encourages staff to spend 15% to 20% of their time working on projects of their choice; other companies like Apple, Facebook, and Johnson & Johnson are all global corporations recognized for their success in CE.

While the terms *entrepreneurship* and *CE* are mostly associated with private sector activity, in the past 30 years the value creation logic has been extended to public sector entrepreneurship (governpreneurship) and more recently social entrepreneurship. Public sector and social organizations worldwide are faced with their greatest challenge in decades. Public sector entrepreneurship is a means of achieving more efficient, flexible, and adaptable management in times of uncertainty and change. This can lead to more intensive and extensive innovations in the management of the public sector organization. The underlying drive for public sector entrepreneurship is the generation of new sources of revenue and the provision of enhanced services to create value for citizens.

Social entrepreneurship can make a significant contribution to communities and society in general by adopting business models to offer innovative and creative solutions to complex social issues. Social entrepreneurship can be broadly defined as innovative activity with a social objective in the for-profit sector—for example, social commercial ventures, nonprofit sector, or across sectors for example hybrid structural forms which combine for-profit and nonprofit approaches. The core objective of public sector and social entrepreneurship is to create value for citizens, stakeholders, and the wider community by utilizing available resources to exploit opportunities that will generate revenue.

While the definitions view the entrepreneurship, CE, public sector entrepreneurship, and social entrepreneurship somewhat distinctive, they include similar concepts such as discovering and exploiting of opportunities, innovating, organizing, creating, rewarding, and risk taking. Entrepreneurs and entrepreneurship is recognized in all professions, industries, and sectors. One all-inclusive broad definition of entrepreneurship and CE is that it is the process of creativity and innovation by committing the necessary time and energy, taking responsibility for all the risks and uncertainties, and taking personal satisfaction.

It must be recognized that there are important differences in the strategies, goals, objectives, restrictions, and results associated with successful entrepreneurship. Well-known entrepreneurs of the 21st century such as Richard Branson (Virgin Group), Michael Dell (Dell), Bill Gates (Microsoft), Kwon Oh Hyun (Samsung), the late Steven Jobs and currently Tim Cook (Apple), Anita Roddick (The Body Shop), and Mark Zuckerberg (Facebook) have all faced different challenges and obstacles along the way, but the one thing they have all demonstrated is commitment and perseverance to their core goals and objectives. The importance of entrepreneurship cannot be overemphasized in the value that it creates for individuals, organizations, and society at large. Entrepreneurship impacts employment, competitiveness, economic growth, and prosperity in a country.

The Meaning of Entrepreneurship to Different Groups

Entrepreneurship can have different meanings for different groups of individuals. Economists, psychologists, sociologists, anthropologists, managers, and businesspeople view entrepreneurship differently from their own perspective:

- Economists—an entrepreneur brings about innovation and change; he or she utilizes resources, labor, materials, and other assets in ways that generate greater value and wealth.
- Psychologists—an entrepreneur is motivated by certain factors—the need to achieve, to experiment, to acquire, or to control his or her own destiny.
- Sociologists—an entrepreneur is typically influenced by his or her culture and community, and the presence or absence of certain conditions motivate or de-motivate individuals for taking up entrepreneurial venture activities either as a start-up or within a large corporation.
- Anthropologists—an entrepreneur is one who recognizes opportunities. The result and the level of entrepreneurial activity is determined by opportunity structure. Opportunity structure is the economic opportunity and ability of entrepreneurs to recognize and act upon such opportunities.
- Managers and Businesspeople—an entrepreneur is an innovator who introduces new ideas for products, services, processes, or markets. To some business owners/managers, an entrepreneur seems to be a threat, a major competitor. To other business owners/ managers, an entrepreneur may be one to unite with, a customer/ client who generates wealth for him or herself and others, identifies

ways to effectively utilize resources, and creates opportunities and employment.

There is no common theoretical framework that synthesizes the diverse views and opinions. Therefore, a valuable and multidimensional number of entrepreneurship theories can be utilized together to describe entrepreneurial phenomena. However, an overlapping theme is that entrepreneurs have a high level of creativity and innovation together with a high level of opportunity recognition, risk taking, visionary activity, and persistence.

Innovation—Meaning and Importance

Innovation is a process that starts with an idea; proceeds with the development of an invention; and results in the development or enhancement of products, services, processes, or technological advancement as part of organizational innovativeness. Innovativeness reflects an inclination to participate in and facilitate new ideas and develop new processes, thereby moving away from existing practices, processes, and technologies. Innovative organizations place a strong emphasis on research and development (R & D). Innovation is not only the opening of new markets but also new ways of serving established and mature markets.

Innovative organizations support new ideas and are experimental and creative—in search of new improved practices and technologies. The newness can be anything from a new product/process to a new distribution system or approach for developing a new organizational system. Examples of these entrepreneurs include Edward Harriman, who reorganized the Union Pacific Railroad through the Northern Pacific Trust and John Pierpont Morgan, who developed his large banking house by reorganizing and financing the nation's industries. The most successful entrepreneurial organizations are those that link knowledge gained from their previous innovations into future innovation strategies.

Innovation, as an act of introducing something new, novel, or advanced with the intention of creating benefit, is one of the most challenging tasks for an organization. It is not just the ability to create, conceptualize, and develop but also the ability to fully recognize the importance of all factors in the internal and external environment. The internal and external factors vary between different sectors and industries and every organization needs to have a comprehensive knowledge and awareness of each aspect of the internal and external environment and the direct and indirect impact that the environment places on their innovation (see Chapters 4 and 6). Successful innovation under complexity, uncertainty, and dynamism can only succeed through collaborative approaches that fully integrate internal and external organizational knowledge. This has influenced organizations to start recognizing that they need to find new ways of determining the knowledge needed to adjust to a continuously complex, uncertain, and dynamic environment. Organizations need new ways of recognizing what knowledge they acquire by discovering, experimenting, and networking with individuals internal and external to the organization. This has led to the rise in what Henry Chesbrough termed *open innovation,* which is linked to the idea core capability and how that influences an organization's innovation process. Moving from internal R & D to external connection and development creates opportunities for SMEs and large corporations to move beyond their core capabilities to retain competitiveness in today's fast-changing environment.

Traditionally, innovation has been more associated with private sector where the driving force to successfully innovate or the application of new innovations in a given industry is fundamental to future growth and development. Innovation is equally important to the private sector organizations, public sector organizations, and social enterprises. Private sector innovativeness is concerned with the creation or development of any product, service, or process for the business that will lead to competitive success. Innovativeness in the public sector is more focused on process improvements, new services, and new organizational forms that will enhance the efficiency and effectiveness in the delivery of services. Innovativeness in social enterprises creates practical, innovative, and sustainable approaches to social problems for the benefit of society in general, mobilizing ideas and resources required for social transformation.

Innovation is central to organizational competitiveness around the globe. Increased competition arising from globalization and technological advancement has heightened companies' needs to leverage and utilize resources to develop innovation within their organization. In today's society, individuals are constantly searching for higher standards of living and the newest, most sophisticated innovations that are introduced such as the iPhone, iPad and iPad Mini, iTunes, eBay, Skype, Viber, and Toyota Hybrid Prius. Increasingly, more sophisticated individual needs necessitate more rapid innovation; this, in turn, intensifies competition. Organizations that fail to innovate will fail to compete and very quickly will fail to exist. Procter and Gamble (P&G) was previously recognized as a company that did not just launch new products but created new product categories; however, in recent years, they have lost their cutting edge in innovation. This has resulted in loss of market share to more competitive and innovative companies like Unilever. Innovation is a key factor in the growth and wealth of organizations and societies. In today's global economy, organizations are only as good as their next innovation and their pipeline of innovations to follow.

Characterizations of Innovation

A common factor in innovation is that it represents something new, whether this is a new product, service, process, or technology. Innovation, whether incremental (improvement to existing product lines) or breakthrough (unique and rare), will result in new ways of doing things and changes the thought process to develop new ways of thinking about things. Innovation in organizations needs to be involved in the following:

- Developing new products, services, processes, or technologies
- Developing new, more efficient methods of production
- Identifying new markets both nationally and globally
- Extending distribution beyond existing channels

Innovation also needs to deliver customer value by creating a product or providing a service that not just meets but exceeds customers' needs, wants, and expectations. Innovations are not always planned or deliberate; some of the most successful innovations were discovered by accident such as cell phones, cornflakes, nylon, penicillin, Post-its, and Teflon. Therefore, organizations need to be open to potential innovations beyond and in contrast to what they are aiming to achieve.

Phases of Innovation

An innovation must progress through a number of phases before it is commercially viable. This applies to all innovations whether incremental or breakthrough in terms of product, service, process, and technological advancement. These phases are as follows:

- Idea generation
- Selection of most viable idea
- Coalition building to transform the selected idea into reality
- Implementation and commercialization of the developed or new product, service, process, or technology

The Link Between Entrepreneurship and Innovation

Entrepreneurship and innovation are complementary. Entrepreneurship is about identifying new innovations and adapting these innovations to achieve greater competitiveness and enhanced performance. Entrepreneurship and innovation are about having a great idea and the resources to implement. Innovation is a core part of entrepreneurship and a way in which an organization can exploit change as an opportunity for new or developed products, services, processes, or technologies. Innovation is a key function in the entrepreneurial process where new ideas are put into practice. Innovation has been recognized as a central characteristic of the entrepreneurial endeavor and one of the most pressing challenges facing organizations today. Innovation harnesses the creative energy and develops those ideas into realistic opportunities. Drucker (1985) stated, "Innovation is the specific function of entrepreneurship.... It is the means by which the entrepreneur either creates new wealth producing resources or endows existing resources with enhanced potential for creating wealth" (p. 43). An entrepreneurial organization is characterized by its degree of innovativeness.

Entrepreneurial mind-sets are continually refining ways to produce and deliver existing goods and services or develop new products, services, or technologies. Entrepreneurship and innovation are linked to each other and interact to help an organization to develop and grow. Both require creative thinking and the desire to think outside the box and take risks. Creativity needs to be managed and ideas need to be transformed into innovations. External environmental forces such as technological advancements, globalization, government deregulation, social changes, and economic downturn require organizations to become more entrepreneurial and innovative than they were in the past.

Entrepreneurship, Innovation, and Organizational Performance

Entrepreneurship and innovation are dynamic processes that enhance organizational performance. Entrepreneurship and innovation can improve the organization's profitability, enhance its growth, deliver competitive advantage, and improve its performance. Organizations that know how to facilitate entrepreneurship and innovation in its various forms are more competitive and perform better than those that do not. Entrepreneurship and innovation can result in the development of important capabilities that can not only improve the organization's financial performance but also produce other nonfinancial outcomes such as experiencing growth in employment, retaining key employees, managing change, and strategic repositioning (see Chapter 10).

Entrepreneurship, Innovation, and the Economy

Entrepreneurship and innovation play a key role in the economy by establishing firms and developing existing ones that in turn create markets and opportunities that contribute to economic growth, development, prosperity, and competitiveness. Entrepreneurs are responsible for a substantial amount of technological innovations driving economic transformation and international trade. Schumpeter (1911/1963) established conceptually the "entrepreneur as innovator" and as a major contributor in driving economic growth and development. Schumpeter's theory predicted that an increase in the number of entrepreneurs leads to an increase in economic growth. Pre-20th-century writing on economic history offers a detailed affirmation that entrepreneurship is critical to long-term economic growth and prosperity (see Chapter 10).

The link between the entrepreneur and market is evident in the example of Amazon.com. Entrepreneur Jeffrey Bezos established the organization, which created major online markets for a board range of products. The link between the entrepreneur and organizations is evident in the example of Intel. Entrepreneurs and founders Bob Noyce and Gordon Moore grew into an organization with over 90,000 employees within 40 years of its foundation. Economic equilibrium, such as prices, distribution of goods, and transaction structure, is influenced by the degree of entrepreneurship and innovation within an economy. The actions of entrepreneurial and innovative organizations are a fundamental driver that brings the economy toward equilibrium.

The Benefits of Entrepreneurship and Innovation to an Economy

There are significant benefits of entrepreneurship and innovation to a society and to allow an economy to flourish. These benefits include the following:

- Generating employment
- Creating wealth
- Introducing new products, services, processes, and technologies

- Opening new industries and markets
- Creating regional development
- Increasing exports
- Intensifying competitiveness
- Creating innovations that can improve the quality of life and well being
- Providing greater customer value
- Generating greater customer choice

Entrepreneurial and innovative organizations have the ability to marshal resources to seize new business opportunities and promote a more productive economy, the foundation for economic growth and development. Identifying these opportunities is more achievable for organizations that keep themselves flexible, because these are the organizations that quickly adapt to change and take advantage of opportunities as they emerge.

A Framework for Managing Entrepreneurship and Innovation

Managing entrepreneurship and innovation has been of increasing interest in recent years by academics, managers, entrepreneurs, individuals, and companies. Innovativeness is the first dimension that characterizes an entrepreneur and an entrepreneurial organization. Innovation is the extent that things are being done that are unique, or different.

While innovation is fundamental to business success, it is challenging for small businesses as well as large corporations to manage and effectively plan. With the increase in globalization and competitive intensity for organizations, the ability to continuously develop successful, competitive innovative products, services, processes, and strategies is essential. There is an ever-increasing need for organizations to become more innovative and engage in entrepreneurial activities to stay ahead.

This book focuses on the important topic of effectively managing entrepreneurship and innovation. An integrative framework of managing entrepreneurship and innovation has been developed. As indicated in Figure 1.1, the framework has four major components: (1) Discovering the Origins of Innovation and Entrepreneurship; (2) Managing Innovation and Entrepreneurship; (3) Operationalizing Innovation and Entrepreneurship; and (4) Making It All Happen: The Future of Innovation and Entrepreneurship.

The starting point is to develop an in-depth understanding of managing entrepreneurship and innovation. Entrepreneurship and innovation are

Figure 1.1 A Framework for Managing Entrepreneurship and Innovation

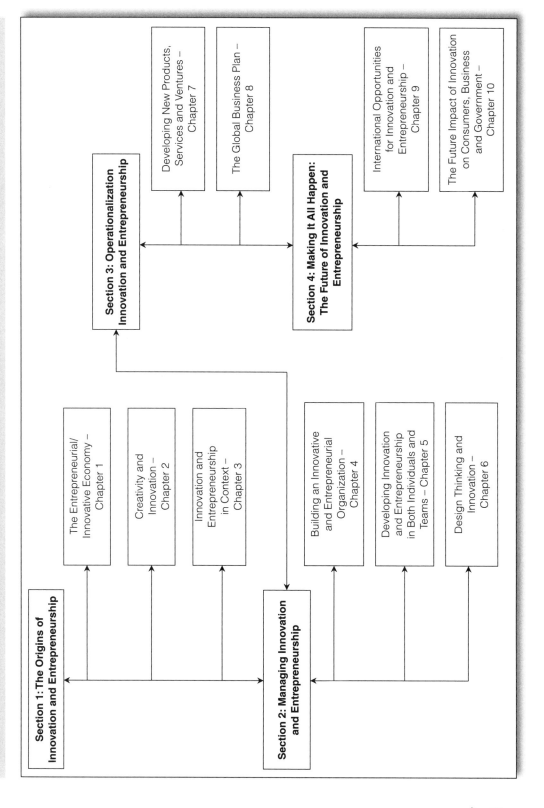

universal concepts, and there are certain commonalities as well as fundamental differences. Building on this foundation, organizational managers must develop and build an organizational environment that encourages and motivates employees to identify and recognize opportunities and behave like entrepreneurs by engaging in innovative activities that will make their organization more competitive and enhance organizational performance.

Three key elements for the origins of innovation and entrepreneurship include (1) understanding entrepreneurship and innovation and the contribution it can make to organizational performance, (2) recognizing the key role and nature of creativity and innovation, and (3) having a clear understanding of the importance of entrepreneurship and innovation within the different contexts. The ability to effectively manage innovation and entrepreneurship requires building an innovative and entrepreneurial organization, developing innovation and entrepreneurship internally among individuals and teams, being able to effectively manage innovation and entrepreneurship in dynamic and uncertain environments, and recognizing and appreciating the importance of design thinking.

Operationalizing innovation and entrepreneurship requires understanding of the aspects of the business plan, the application of tools and techniques, as well as an appropriate organization to support innovation and entrepreneurship and an explicit process to manage the development of new products, services, and ventures. Finally, making it happen—the future of innovation and entrepreneurship—requires understanding the international opportunities for innovation and entrepreneurship, which allows organizations of all sizes to become more competitive and establishing innovation and entrepreneurship in your organization in times of global economic prosperity or global economic downturn.

Section 1 of this book, Discovering the Origins of Innovation and Entrepreneurship, consisting of Chapters 1 through 3, provides the origins of innovation and entrepreneurship. The chapters highlight the core benefits of entrepreneurship and innovation and the way it can improve organizational performance. This requires individuals and groups identifying, evaluating, and selecting particular opportunities for developing the organization and improving its profitability and success. Creativity and innovation are examined by investigating the approaches, role, and nature of the creative process. In light of the importance of innovation and entrepreneurship, the different types of innovation, the innovation process, and sources of innovation in small and medium enterprises (SMEs) and large corporations are presented.

Section 2 of the book, Managing Innovation and Entrepreneurship, consisting of Chapters 4 through 6, focuses on the management of innovation and entrepreneurship. An innovative and entrepreneurial organization requires an appropriate structure, system, and management orientation. Developing an innovative organizational culture with appropriate structures and processes is fundamental. The behaviors associated with innovation and entrepreneurship requires promoting individual and team creativity. A system for monitoring, assessing, and evaluating the external environment to ensure the right decisions are made and actions are taken needs to be established. A discussion of the concept of design thinking and its significance in meeting the needs and demands of customers to achieve business success concludes this section.

Section 3 of the book, Operationalizing Innovation and Entrepreneurship, consisting of Chapters 7 and 8, deals with operationalizing innovation and entrepreneurship. A concerted effort needs to be made to build and plan the innovation case: how it will unfold and develop and how it will be successful. Since developing new products, services, and ventures is a challenge, the most common processes for development, which are the stage gate and development funnel, are explored. How the market influences the process of development and commercialization of breakthrough innovations versus incremental innovations are discussed along with the differences between developing new products and services. Additionally, organizations can develop innovations outside their existing strategy. The section closes with a discussion on the importance and aspects of a business plan such as forecasting the sales and profits of the innovation, assessing and recognizing the risk and uncertainty, and anticipating the necessary human and nonhuman resources needed.

Section 4 of the book, Making It All Happen: The Future of Innovation and Entrepreneurship, consisting of Chapters 9 and 10, is concerned with the future of innovation and entrepreneurship. There are significant differences between an international and a domestic business. With technological advancements today, competitors are anyone your customers have access to. SMEs and large corporations need to think globally. This requires understanding the local factors that influence the level and the direction of innovations. One of the key concerns for managing innovation and entrepreneurship is how to achieve growth. Financial and nonfinancial performance measures of innovation in SMEs and large corporations are discussed. The book concludes with a discussion of the future of innovation on customers, organizations, and governments.

Summary

Entrepreneurship and innovation is not just associated with business start-up but also existing and mature organizations in the private, public, and social sectors. It includes innovations that exist inside or outside the domain of an existing organization. These include innovations such as the creation of new venture, new and novel combinations of existing products, new forms of production, and new markets. There is a greater need for entrepreneurship and innovation today more than ever before due to globalization, technological advancement and development, intensified competitiveness, and the global economic downturn. Entrepreneurship and innovation is important to individuals, organizations, and governments and will continually impact consumers and economic development in the future.

References

Drucker, P. F. (1985). *Innovation and entrepreneurship: Practice and principles*. London: Butterworth-Heinemann.

Hisrich, R., Peters, M., & Shepherd, D. (2012). *Entrepreneurship* (9th ed.). New York: McGraw-Hill.

Schumpeter, J. A. (1963). *The theory of economic development: An inquiry into profits, capital, credit, interest and the business cycle* (R. Opie, Trans.). Oxford, UK: Oxford University Press. (Original work published 1911)

Suggested Readings

Ahlstrom, D. (2010). Innovation and growth: How business contributes to society. *Academy of Management Perspectives, 24*(3), 11–24.

In this article, the author argues that the core business objective is the development of new innovative goods and services that generate economic growth while also providing important societal benefits. The author asserts that small changes in economic growth can create major differences in income; this, in turn, makes firm growth very salient to societies. Through innovation and growth, firms can greatly benefit society.

Finkle, T. A. (2012). Corporate entrepreneurship and innovation in Silicon Valley: The case of Google, Inc. *Entrepreneurship Theory and Practice, 36*(4), 863–884.

In this article, the author provides a case study of Google Inc. The author discusses the problem Google faced in how they could maintain the company's culture of CE and innovation in light of stagnant profits and other key issues. The case focuses on Google seeking answers on how to develop CE and innovation during the most challenging economic climate in the history of the company.

Haynie, J. M., Shepherd, D., Mosakowski, E., & Earley, P. C. (2010). A situated metacognitive model of the entrepreneurial mindset. *Journal of Business Venturing, 25*(2), 217–229.

The authors develop a framework to examine the bases of an "entrepreneurial mind-set," explained by scholars as the ability to sense, act, and mobilize in uncertain conditions. The authors focus on metacognitive processes that allow the entrepreneur to think beyond or reorganize existing knowledge structures and heuristics, promoting adaptable cognitions in light of novel and uncertain decision contexts.

Welter, F. (2011). Contextualizing entrepreneurship: Conceptual challenges and ways forward. *Entrepreneurship Theory and Practice, 35*(1), 165–184.

In this article, the author explores the contexts for entrepreneurship, demonstrating how a contextualized view of entrepreneurship contributes to understanding the phenomenon. In his research, he argues that context is fundamental for understanding when, how, and why entrepreneurship happens and who becomes involved. Exploring the multiplicity of contexts and their impact on entrepreneurship, the author identifies challenges researchers face in contextualizing entrepreneurship theory and makes recommendations for ways forward.

Williams, L., & McGuire, S. (2010). Economic creativity and innovation implementation: The entrepreneurial drivers of growth? Evidence from 63 countries. *Small Business Economics, 34*(4), 391–412.

In this article, the authors examine the impact of culture on national innovation and prosperity. Using a sample of 63 countries, they propose and test a comprehensive explanation of how culture as an umbrella construct affects innovation and national prosperity. Their empirical findings buttress the theoretical arguments that culture powerfully shapes the character of national innovation.

2

Creativity and Innovation

W hat is meant by the term *creativity?* What is the role of
creativity in organizations? What are the key stages of the
creative process? What are the core components of individual
creativity? Is creativity important for innovation to emerge and develop
within organizations? Why? What is the link between creativity and
innovation?

Scenario: Virgin Atlantic Airways

In the early 1980s, Richard Branson was a well-renowned entrepreneur
for Virgin Records. In 1984, he announced the launch of Virgin Atlantic
Airways, an airline that focused on high quality and low cost. On June
22, 1984, Virgin had its inaugural flight from Gatwick Airport in West
Sussex, United Kingdom, to Newark Airport in Newark, New Jersey. The
core objective of the airline was as follows: To provide the highest quality innovative service at excellent value for money for all classes of air
travelers. By the late 1980s, over 1 million passengers had flown with
Virgin Atlantic. Selling Virgin Records to Thorn EMI in 1992, Branson
then invested the proceeds in Virgin Atlantic. Creativity and innovation
continued in the 1990s with purchasing new planes, extending the route
network, and generating greater creativity and innovation in all services
to passengers. To establish a global partnership, Branson sold a 49%
stake in Virgin Atlantic to Singapore Airlines in 1999. Singapore Airlines
paid £600.25 million for this stake, which included a capital injection of
£49 million, and Virgin Atlantic was valued at a minimum of £1.225 billion.
The deal was finalized in early 2000, and Branson continues to hold a
controlling 51% stake in Virgin Atlantic Airways. However, in December

2012, Singapore Airlines sold their 49% stake to Delta Airlines for $360 million (£224m).

Virgin Atlantic Airways is well renowned for its innovations and competitiveness. It provides three classes of travel (Upper Class, Premium Economy, and Economy); all classes offer in-flight entertainment. In March 2006, the new Virgin Atlantic Clubhouse opened at Heathrow Airport. This offered many unique features including a spa, hair salon, brasserie, cocktail bar, and game room. Virgin Atlantic launched a new check-in facility at Heathrow Terminal 3 in 2007. This provided Economy and Premium Economy passengers with a bright, more spacious, and efficient check-in. Passengers travelling Upper Class had access to a private security corridor so they could proceed through the terminal to the clubhouse.

Currently, Virgin Atlantic has 38 aircrafts, which include 13 Boeing 747s, six Airbus A340-300s, and 19 Airbus A340-600s. A pioneering biofuel demonstration was held in 2008 with GE Aviation on a 747 between London and Amsterdam. This was the first-ever commercial airline flight to use biofuel. The Boeing 787-9 Dreamliner is significantly more fuel efficient, burning approximately 27% less fuel per passenger compared to the Airbus A340-300, so Virgin Atlantic ordered 15 of them with the opportunity to order an additional 8 and purchasing rights on 20 more aircraft. Delivery of these planes continues from 2011 until 2014.

Since its founding, Virgin Atlantic Airways has become the second largest British carrier serving major cities around the world. It has carried approximately 53 million passengers and has 9,000 employees worldwide. Virgin Atlantic is based at London's Heathrow and Gatwick airports and Manchester. In the United Kingdom, it is the second-largest long-haul airline and the third largest European carrier over the North Atlantic, operating worldwide long-haul services to 30 destinations. Virgin Atlantic has led the way in the quality of service, which competing airlines aim to follow.

While Virgin Atlantic's has achieved growth, the focus is to ensure that the service is customer driven with clear emphasis on providing good value, high quality, and innovation. Branson's strong entrepreneurial mindset and fearless reputation, such as ballooning across the Atlantic Ocean, has provided Virgin with significant publicity. Additionally, James Bond films *Casino Royale* and *Quantum of Solace* featured the Virgin Atlantic aircraft, resulting in major publicity worldwide. Branson's entrepreneurial attitude combined with the publicity gained has significantly contributed to the international success of the Virgin brand.

In addition to Virgin Atlantic Airways, the Virgin Group has expanded beyond the airline to include international *megastore* music retailing, book and software publishing, film and video editing facilities, clubs, trains,

Virgin.com, and financial advice companies, resulting in more than 100 companies in 15 countries. Branson is a true entrepreneur and innovator. Besides all his business ventures, Branson is a trustee and supporter of a broad range of charities that include the Virgin Healthcare Foundation. "Change for Children Appeal" has raised over £2.75 million in support of worldwide children's healthcare initiatives. Branson also engaged in the development of Charity Projects, which later formed the hugely successful Charity Projects campaign.

With its successful history and leadership from a leading international entrepreneur who is willing to take risks and do what it takes to stay ahead, there is no doubt that Virgin Atlantic Airways will continue to be creative and innovative.

SOURCE: Adapted from www.virgin-atlantic.com.

Introduction

Creativity and innovation are frequently used interchangeably. There are fundamental distinctions between the two concepts that need to be recognized. Creativity is a core building block for innovation. Creativity encompasses the processes leading to the generation of new and valued ideas. Without creativity, there would be no innovation, because creativity is the foundation on which innovation emerges, develops, and grows. Creativity is about developing ideas, processes, or concepts, while innovation is the practical application of those ideas, processes, or concepts. However, everyone can come up with ideas, but creativity and innovation involve ideas, processes, or concepts that are commercially viable. Creativity can lead to inventions, but until they are commercialized, they are not innovations. To be successful, the creativity and innovation must create new value for customers and generate return. One such company is Twitter, which was launched in March 2006 as an online social networking service and microblogging service that allows users to send and read *tweets*. This innovative service has gained popularity among a broad population of celebrities and the general public with over 500 million users as of 2012. Entrepreneurs and entrepreneurial organizations can use creativity to improve what they are currently doing. This is a process of innovation based on existing products or services. Others do things that no one else is doing, and this involves invention of technologies, products, and methods that cause those currently in existence to become obsolete. Survival in a dynamic, competitive environment requires not mimicking and implementing the solutions and approaches of other organizations but opening themselves to new ideas and new ways of doing things. To achieve this, organizations must utilize their resources and the creative abilities of their people.

Creativity and innovation are not possible without people who have the required competencies, motivation, and curiosity to discover and invent something novel. It is the creativity in people and their ideas that produce innovations, but the organization must support and nurture this for their benefit just like 3M allowing 15% and Google allowing 20% of staff time researching selected projects; Dyson and Salesforce.com focus on encouraging and following through on good ideas generated by individuals. The people involved in the creative and innovative process and how they are organized and supported can have significant impact on the organization's innovation performance and its ability to be competitive through innovation. All types of organizations need to be creative and innovate if they are to develop and grow. From an organizational perspective, developing creativity in individuals at all levels strengthens their ability to recognize and take advantage of different opportunities and possibilities. The level of organizational support to facilitate and meet the specific challenges they face in the market can determine how successful they will be. From an individual perspective, when individuals are creative they feel more self-confident and energized. Individuals derive personal satisfaction from being creative, which leads them to be more productive with the possibility of producing breakthrough ideas.

Creativity is a critical skill for recognizing or creating opportunity in a dynamic environment. Creativity in products, services, and processes is now more important than ever due to globalization and increased competitiveness. It is just as important in the established enterprise, the public sector organization, and the new venture. Creativity and creative organizations are the success stories of the 21st century. A creative business like Virgin Atlantic Airways that is willing to take risks and works on its mission and strategy to keep ahead of competition is the key to achieving competitive advantage in a highly dynamic and uncertain market. Dawning Information Industry proved its creativity and innovation in October 2011 by building the world's fastest supercomputer, which performed 2.57 quadrillion calculations per second. Dawning's technology has pushed the company's supercomputer market share past IBM's and Hewlett-Packard's (HP) in China.

The purpose of this chapter is to examine the ways organizations can prosper through creativity and innovation. The chapter discusses creativity and innovation by providing an understanding of what creativity is and its contribution to innovation. It develops an understanding of the creative process and discusses the creative techniques. Furthermore, it recognizes that creativity is a complex and continuous process and not just a one-time implementation. This is followed by the appreciation that creativity can be nurtured and developed in an organization through individual creative competencies and organizational development of creativity and innovation. The chapter concludes with a discussion on the link between creativity and innovation.

What Is Creativity?

Creativity is the core of innovation and is necessary to develop innovative business concepts. It is fundamental for identifying the patterns and trends that define an opportunity. While there are numerous perspectives including psychological, social, individual, and organizational, creativity is the application of an individual's ability to identify and develop new ideas, processes, or concepts in novel ways. It is the act of relating previously unrelated things in novel and useful ways—a deviation from conventional perspectives. Both novelty and usefulness are necessary conditions for an idea to be considered creative. These ideas, processes, or concepts must be useful and have value or meaning. Netflix is a highly creative company that recognized an opportunity and capitalized on the success of the DVD and the booming Internet-streaming service. It was established in 1997 and since then has become a $9 billion powerhouse (crushing Blockbuster). Netflix has been one of the most successful dot-com ventures. Despite a series of hurdles that Netflix faced since July 2011, it was launched in the United Kingdom and Ireland on January 9, 2012. Creativity requires perseverance, passion, and commitment—all of which is demonstrated by the leading companies such as 3M, Apple, Amazon, Facebook, Google, Salesforce.com, Samsung, Twitter, and Virgin Atlantic Airways.

Individuals are inherently creative and have the capability to find and solve complex problems. While some continuously act on their creativity, others are not always aware of their creative ability. As a result, many fail to recognize when and how creative they are being and therefore miss out on opportunities for creativity arising within their day-to-day work activities. When creative behaviors are harnessed among individuals with diverse skills and perspectives, creativity can be unique and useful in leading to successful innovations.

There is no one idea of creativity that is appropriate for all endeavors. Creativity requires both cognitive and noncognitive skills, inquisitiveness, intuition, and determination. Creative solutions can be created or discovered immediately or over long periods of time. Creativity is not just a revolutionary changing product that comes from world-renowned innovators like Alexander Graham Bell, Thomas Edison, Albert Einstein, Sigmund Freud, or more recently James Dyson, the late Steve Jobs, or Mark Zuckerberg. Creativity is the ability to consistently produce different and valuable results. A key aspect in producing valuable outcomes is commitment and focus to channel creativity and achieve desirable results in light of potential limitations.

Creativity is a process that can lead to incremental improvements or breakthrough innovations. While breakthrough innovations such as penicillin, the computer, and the automobile are great, most innovations make incremental improvements to existing product lines rather than risk bringing something radically new to market. Technological innovations such as voice and text messaging and the jet airplane occur more frequently than breakthrough innovations and are, in general, at a lower level of scientific discovery and advancement. Incremental innovation is the form of innovation that occurs most frequently. It usually extends a technological innovation into a better product or service with a different and usually greater market appeal. American Express is always looking to extend, modify, and enhance its services. Apple's successful innovations include the iPhone and the iPad. But the core innovation for Apple is the platforms that have facilitated an ecosystem of creativity—from gaming to finance to chip making. Apple's innovations have changed the life, work, and world of millions. Apple, with the legendary late Steve Jobs (former CEO), is one of the most innovative companies of the century. Google Inc. was formed in 1997. Their innovation (and enterprise) is at the core of their strategy. Google has grown substantially. Initially providing single language search options, they now offer numerous products and services, as well as a variety of advertising and web applications for all task variations, in many languages. Google has been transformed from a single product into a diversified web power. Facebook (see Chapter 1) is a social networking site that created a breakthrough innovation by creating a new culture that changed the way people communicate. Facebook now has over 1.06 billion users worldwide. General Electric has a drive to invent and be innovative where it matters most in areas such as electronic medical records, innovative new power generation that reduces emissions, and Water Explorer for Google Earth. 3M captures the essence of new innovative ideas and transforms them into ingenious products such as the famous Post-it Notes, 3M stain resistant additives and sealers, 3M Mobile Projector MP225a, 3M Unitek Incognito Lite Appliance System. Samsung combines innovation with green technology; they are moving fast and furious with innovative products such as Galaxy S Duos and Galaxy S III Mini. These companies have been able to continuously innovate and transform themselves to serve new and growing markets by developing innovative products and delivering them effectively. Creativity and innovation does not just happen; it requires both general knowledge and field-specific knowledge, because creative individuals cannot know what is novel without an understanding of existing knowledge in any specific area. Additionally, without this knowledge, they cannot harness the creative energy and develop those ideas into realistic products, processes, or services.

If an organization is bringing about creativity through innovative products, services, and technologies that satisfy customers' needs, wants, and expectations; creates employment; and contributes to economic growth and development—or alternatively the organization is the local government creatively utilizing ideas to meet the needs of the wider community and therefore improving the standard of living—creativity and innovation play a key role in serving members of society.

Creativity can range from low levels to relatively high levels. Lower level creativity frequently involves incremental modifications and adjustments of an existing idea or a combination of two or more previously unrelated ideas in a novel and useful way. Higher level creativity involves more breakthrough contributions. There are different forms of creativity:

- Creativity that develops new ideas, processes, or concepts
- Creativity that modifies existing ideas, processes, or concepts. See these examples:
  - Creates a new, improved version that is more efficient and effective
  - Adds additional features and functions
  - Performs in a different setting
  - Targets a new audience
- Creativity that combines things that were previously unrelated.

Whether creativity is entirely new, modified, or a combination of previously unrelated things, it is a process of developing novel and useful ideas, processes, or concepts. Creativity and innovation need people who are willing and eager to utilize their core competencies in the most creative and innovative ways. Being creative involves the following:

- Open-mindedness and objectiveness
- Perseverance and dedication to continuously seek and produce ideas
- An ability to put existing or new ideas together in different ways
- Drive and ability to overcome obstacles or find alternative solutions

- Moderate risk taker
- Intrinsic motivation
- Internal locus of control
- Desire to achieve and grow
- Driven by growth and development

The Creative Process

Creativity is originality that is realistic, viable, and marketable. Three key aspects of organizational creativity are (1) *knowledge,* (2) *drive,* and (3) *ability.* Knowledge of the course of action is required for opportunity identification, problem solving, and decision making. Drive refers to the passion, desire, and motivation to do something new and novel with the confidence to proceed as a first mover. This individual has an internal locus of control and is driven by a sense of achievement and self-fulfillment. Ability refers to the ways in which an individual seeks to identify a solution to a problem by adopting diverse and creative techniques in order to accurately assess and evaluate the situation and identify the best and most viable course of action. The following five components are the essential aspects of the creative process:

1. Preparation

2. Incubation

3. Illumination

4. Validation

5. Implementation

Preparation

Preparation is the background, experience, and knowledge that an individual brings to the opportunity recognition process. It is through the preparation stage that the individual attempts to find answers to the question, problem, or challenge. At this stage, it is important to fully understand the issue in order to have the required knowledge to find the best possible solution.

Incubation

Incubation is the stage where an individual considers an idea or thinks about a problem. Time and space are necessary to reflect on the solution or considerations that may not be immediately forthcoming. The incubation stage frequently occurs when individuals are involved in activities totally unrelated to the question, problem, or challenge. This stage is valuable as it is important to identify where extra help may be needed in order to progress forward.

Illumination

The illumination stage involves the individual coming up with an outline of an answer to the question, problem, or challenge. Frequently this answer needs to be further refined and modified.

Validation

The individual tries to select the choice with a calculated level of risk and uncertainty. The ultimate success of the chosen alternative depends on whether it can be translated into action. This stage often requires further modification and adjustments to fit the organizational culture. At this stage, the idea is subject to scrutiny and analyzed for its viability. This is a particularly challenging stage of the creative process because it requires the individual to objectively reflect on the viability of the idea.

Implementation

Implementation involves the use of managerial, administrative, and persuasive abilities to ensure that the selected alternative is carried out effectively. This is the transformation of the creative idea into reality.

Innovation occurs through cycles of divergent creative thinking, which brings about many potential alternatives followed by convergence to a selected solution. Divergence is breaking from the normal and familiar ways of doing things. It is focused on coming up with new ideas and solutions. It expands the number of potential solutions through the process of creativity. It is the most dynamic and social phase and underpins the creative process. Convergence is the achievement of some agreement regarding the benefits of a given idea and the value in pursuing that idea. It removes any nonviable options. It is an assessment in terms of the implementation issues. Unless the convergence stage is well managed, the most viable and innovative ideas may be lost. Creativity depends on a repeated cycle of divergence and convergence to first create a diversity of options and then determine the best ideas to implement. This process takes time and depends on the question, problem, or challenge that the organization is facing. The creative process involves both logical and analytical thinking in the preparation, validation, and implementation stages. In addition, it calls for imagining, using intuition, conceptualizing, and synthesizing in the incubation and illumination stages.

Creative Techniques

While creativity is recognized as being important, it is rarely exploited to its full potential. Creativity can be enhanced through practice. For creative outcomes to be produced and developed, individuals must be trained in creative techniques. Innovative and entrepreneurial organizations recognize that everyone throughout the organization needs to contribute their experience and creativity. Creative tools provide a structured approach for an individual, group, or team to utilize and combine their intuition, drive, imagination, and experience to develop an idea or concept that is useful and eventually applied into practice. These innovative solutions can be applied to virtually any organization in any sector:

- Developing new products, processes, or services
- Increasing efficiency and effectiveness through the production process
- Meeting the needs, wants, and expectations of customers
- Being environmentally friendly—reducing cost and waste

There are numerous techniques available for the generation of creative ideas and concepts. A useful way of categorizing the techniques is on the relative amounts of structure and the role in focusing (convergence) or extending (divergence) options. One well-known creative technique is *brainstorming*, where a team of approximately 6 to 12 members generate a large volume of ideas without criticism and then evaluate each idea. *Brainwriting* is a silent version of brainstorming where the generated ideas are recorded individually on a piece of paper and submitted anonymously to the group. The ideas are exchanged a number of times with each person building on the previously generated ideas. *Focus groups* include individuals providing information in a structured format. *Free association* is writing down a word or phrase related to the problem, followed by another and another, with the goal that each new word will add something new to the ongoing thought processes and, thereby generating a chain of ideas, finishing with the emergence of a new product idea. *Mind mapping* allows an individual or team to generate numerous ideas by dividing each idea into many more detailed ideas. *Collection notebook method* is when individuals or teams consider the problem and potential solutions, recording ideas at least once but ideally three times daily. After a week, the best ideas are listed, as well as any suggestions. *Problem inventory analysis* is a method for generating new ideas and opportunities by focusing on existing problems.

The value of these techniques depends on the individual's thinking process, problem-solving ability, and decision making. The thinking process is usually better if participants have diverse perspectives, backgrounds, experiences, skills, and expertise; this avoids *groupthink* and enhances out-of-the-box thinking. The goal of creative techniques is to manage creativity in a more systematic way and improve the quality of the creative output, resulting in a high quality concept or solution.

Components of Individual Creativity

Individuals are frequently unconscious of the fact that they are being creative. Creativity can be quickly enhanced where individuals recognize the ways in which they are being creative, understand their own potential, and adopt systematic approaches for engaging that potential. Creative approaches must be viable and useful in the context of an organization and its competitive environment. Amabile's (1998) work has focused on three ingredients for creative output: (1) expertise, (2) creative-thinking skills, and (3) motivation. Taking Amabile's (1998) work as the foundation, there are four important components of successful creativity in an organization:

1. Knowledge, skills, and expertise—individual competencies that can explore opportunities and develop creative approaches to problem solving. Knowledge, skills, and experience are the foundation for all creative work.

2. Drive, motivation, and perseverance—individual passion and desire to do something new and novel. Studies have found that intrinsic motivation (driven by active participation in the work, inquisitiveness, contentment, or a sense of challenge) makes a greater contribution to creativity than extrinsic motivation (driven by the desire to achieve a goal outside of the actual work, such as winning a competition or receiving a reward).

3. Creative thinking and discovery—individual ability to think outside the box. Creative thinking and discovery to some extent is influenced by personality characteristics associated with self-discipline,

self-confidence, independence, risk taking, accept ambiguity, and determination in light of challenges.

4. Flexibility and support—individual ability to seek and utilize the resources and support necessary to develop useful ideas or concepts. Being able to utilize the resources that are available within the working environment contributes to the development of individual creativity.

The key components of creativity are connected where each one influences the other (see Figure 2.1). Individual's knowledge, skills, and expertise, along with his or her drive, motivation, perseverance, creative thinking, discovery ability, flexibility, and support where they can effectively seek and utilize the resources and support necessary to develop useful ideas or concepts, can make a significant contribution to the long-term creative results in an organization and in turn their innovativeness.

Figure 2.1 Components of Individual Creativity

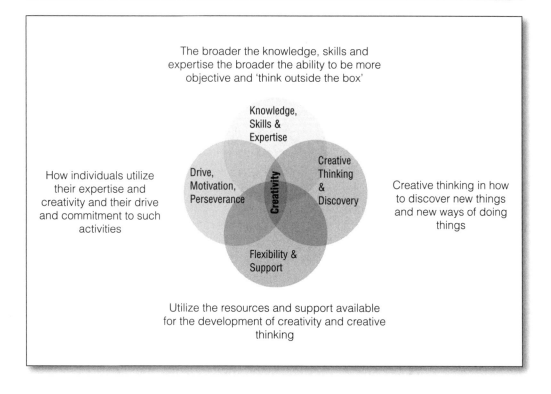

Creative individuals have the drive, motivation, and perseverance in their work. The utilization of their existing competencies combined with this drive, motivation, and perseverance is central to the creative accomplishment of invention and discovery. Nissan's true innovation emerged with CEO Carlos Ghosn's perseverance and commitment to invest in new, unproven all-electric technology. Ghosn's risk with the Leaf has created the lead for Nissan in the competition for genuine sustainable transportation. Individual's confidence and ability to deal with the success and failures of discovery and invention combined with the organizational support and facilitation to embrace successes and learn from failures are important components of creativity. The more supportive the organization, the more confident individuals are in tapping into their creative side and generating viable ideas and concepts. Organizations need to create a supportive nonthreatening, noncontrolling environment, which is necessary for the generation of ideas. Salesforce.com is a very successful Cloud Computing Company whose CEO Marc Benioff focuses on getting new ideas by talking to different people, experimenting, and asking questions to promote the status quo and generate new ideas. He encourages everyone to bring about new ideas and utilizes creativity and innovation from his human resources. Entrepreneurs and organizational managers determine the internal organizational environment and have the opportunities to foster creativity leading to successful innovations such as James Dyson who encourages creativity and takes the suggestions of people within the organization very seriously—following through on the good ideas generated, which also helps attract creative risk takers to the company. Effective entrepreneurs and organizational managers not only encourage creativity among workers but are creative and innovative themselves. They act as innovators in the way they recruit, promote people, generate ideas from the top to the bottom of the organization as well as externally. They are willing to accept failure as a natural part of creativity and innovation. They know that creativity and innovation is a key to future success and they make it part of the organization. Entrepreneurs and organizational managers can engage in the following:

- Modeling: Share their thinking with staff at all levels; explain how they create or combine ideas, and provide a supportive environment and the necessary resources to do so.
- Communicating expectations: Let staff at all levels know that creative ideas are encouraged and recognized.
- Reinforcing: Commend creative thinking, particularly when the idea fails.

Organizational Creativity and Innovation

Highly creative and innovative organizations recognize that creativity and innovation cannot be assigned to a selected number of individuals. Creativity and innovation must be fostered throughout the organization and be part of its culture. Organizations must become creative and innovative across the entire spectrum of business activities; this requires participation of all employees at all levels.

While individual, team, and organizational inhibitions combined with external environmental pressures accumulate and can restrict creative potential and actions. The issue for the organization is to manage this in a way that creates an environment that allows creativity to flourish and contribute to effective innovation. Management needs to understand all aspects of the internal and external environment that supports creativity along with the more severe aspects that inhibit creativity. It is therefore important to invest in research and development (R & D) and spend time exploring creative ideas and opportunities rather than make quick decisions that are not adequately thought out. It is also important not to spend too much time over analyzing and miss out on important innovations. All types of organizations from small and medium enterprises (SMEs), large corporations, and national and multinational companies in the private, public, or social sector need to be creative and innovative if they are to survive and grow. Procter and Gamble (P&G) is an example of a highly innovative company despite the challenges that they have faced a decade ago with only 15% of innovation initiatives being successful. More recently, they have not had any major innovations and new product development. Now P&G has the new-growth factory, which is focused on systematizing the pursuit of growth through innovation (Brown & Scott, 2011). No company can stand still in today's dynamic environment, and every company needs to engage in innovation in order to survive. While many SMEs and large corporations do not have the resources of P&G, they can adopt their approach by first pursuing growth through innovation and then doing things better and differently to meet the demands of consumers' in today's very challenging environment. Innovation should be important to every organization; therefore, leaders must invest time to establish and nurture innovation throughout the organization. There are particular skills that separate business innovators like Jeff Bezos, the late Steve Jobs, and Marc Benioff from ordinary managers. These skills include observing, experimenting, networking, questioning, and thinking outside the box. Leaders can change their behavior to improve their creative impact.

Creativity resulting in innovation occurs through a knowledge and comprehension of the external environment and the ability to recognize opportunities through the interplay of the individual characteristics and competencies and organizational climate (see Figure 2.2). In building a creative organization, attention needs to be focused on three core areas. The first is the *external environment;* collecting and processing information about the trends emerging within the external environment is needed in order to fully understand potential opportunities and threats that the internal environment may face. The second is *individual characteristics* and *individual competencies.* Individuals need to have the required characteristics to be creative. They need to be motivated, open-minded, and objective as well as demonstrate a willingness to take risks and be proactive. They must have a clear understanding of creativity and problem-solving tools as well as core competencies and intuition that enhance their creativity and help them solve problems. The third is the *organizational climate,* and its environment needs to be evaluated to define opportunities for creative performance. This means an organizational climate needs to be created that does not just support creativity and innovation but has it deeply engrained in its very

Figure 2.2 Organizational Creativity for Innovation

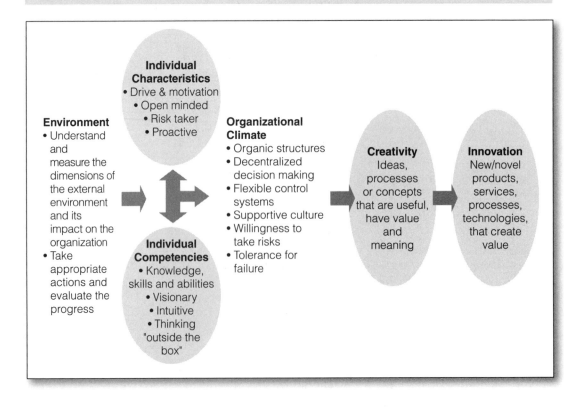

existence. There are many aspects of the organizational climate that influence creativity and innovation, but the most influential ones are structures, decentralized decision making, flexible control systems, supportive culture, willingness to take risks, and tolerance for failure.

Creativity is a function of individual characteristics and competencies. Similarly, organizational creativity is a function of the creative outcomes from individuals, contextual influences, and external environmental factors. The overall outcome in terms of new products, processes, or services is a consequence of the interaction among the individual, organization, and external environment.

What Makes An Organization Creative?

The way an organization is structured to meet the specific challenges faced in the market can determine their level of success. The way organizations approach tasks and activities is an indicator of their attitude toward creativity and innovation. Highly creative organizations adapt to the needs of the external environment efficiently and effectively. To achieve this, they rely on a wide variety of sources of information and knowledge to drive the organization forward through creative and innovative actions. They encourage new ideas and challenge employees to think broadly and long term. Highly creative organizations place a strong emphasis on creativity and innovation and the alignment to their long-term goals and objectives. These organizations allow employees the freedom and flexibility in how they achieve their strategic goals. Highly creative organizations respect and value individualism and diverse opinions. They value consensus but not at the expense of groupthink. The level of control they place upon employees does not stifle initiative, as individuals are given scope to define and undertake their job. This satisfies the individual's need to have influence about how they work towards achieving their task. Highly creative organizations know that not every initiative can produce a positive outcome, and they create an environment where failure is tolerated.

The Link Between Creativity and Innovation

The link between innovation and creativity can be broken into three stages. The first stage comprises creativity through idea, activity, ability, and skill. The second stage comprises invention through working model and prototype. The final sage comprises innovation through successful commercial introduction of the invention.

Creativity is a process of generating ideas, and innovation is the refinement and implementation of those ideas. Creativity alone is not sufficient. Innovation is necessary to take the new or existing creative ideas and put them into action. It is the development, approval, and implementation of new ideas, products, services, or processes. Within the context of the organization, the focus is on bringing a creative idea to fruition. From an organizational perspective, many great ideas just never manifest beyond that "great idea." Ideas that are brought to market must be acknowledged for their potential, have the necessary funding, and possess the ability to overcome obstacles such as competitiveness, technological challenges, and economic uncertainty. This is known as the innovation process, and it is a fundamental process when referring to organizational creativity. Epocrates is an example of a company that has created innovation by providing doctors and nurses with instant drug reference through a program for mobiles and laptops. With the click of a button, the program allows medical professionals to make accurate prescribing decisions.

Creativity without innovation has no real value. Similarly, without creative ideas to initiate the innovation so it can develop and grow, innovation cannot accelerate. "Thus, no innovation is possible without the creative processes that mark the front end of the process: identifying important problems and opportunities, gathering information, generating new ideas, and exploring the validity of those ideas" (Amabile, 2004, p. 1).

Creativity is initiated at the individual level. Individual creativity is related to factors such as personality, motivation, competency, and expertise. At the organizational level, environmental factors such as culture and climate affect creativity and therefore influence the behavior of individuals. The lack or insufficiency in creativity and innovation is one of the biggest threats to organizations today. Organizations such as 3M, Apple, American Greetings, Google, and Virgin Group practice creativity by looking more broadly for ideas within their industries rather than where everyone else is looking. Future opportunities are typically about being able to differentiate from what everyone else is doing and link creative ideas into innovations that are commercially viable and generate value.

Summary

Creativity is essentially the development of novel ideas—predominately at the individual level. Innovation is the process whereby those ideas are selected, evaluated, and supported in terms of funding and resources; developed; and promoted with the objective of achieving successful commercialization. Creativity is the first step in innovation, which is the successful implementation of the best and most commercially viable ideas. Creativity plays a key role in innovation in the way it is fundamental in developing ideas and solutions as well as installing and implementing the selected solution. Innovation is fundamental for an organization's long-term success and cannot happen without creativity.

Creativity brings with it a new start, a new approach, freedom, flexibility, and a sense of what can be achieved. Creativity happens intentionally or unintentionally, and individuals are frequently unconscious of the fact that they are being creative or the potential value of their creativity. To be creative is to have an effect, to make a difference, and to add value. Creativity and innovation depend on the individual and the collective competencies of employees at all levels within the organization. Organizational managers need to manage creativity and innovation. They must manage individuals and teams by creating an environment that continuously generates creative ideas and utilizes its innovation process to identify the value of those ideas. This can be done through a broad range of processes, such as creative techniques, as well as ensure that the right structures and systems are in place that provides individuals and teams with the flexibility, support, and scope for creative performance in their day-to-day work activities.

The business world is more dynamic and uncertain with the pace of change rapidly accelerating. Organizations need to change accordingly if they are to survive and grow. For an organization to be competitive and achieve its goals, management must keep focused on the external environment in which they operate, and in developing and implementing their innovations, they must meet and exceed the demands of their customers. Organizations that implement new ideas that are focused on this dynamic and changing global environment are likely to succeed and thrive.

Creativity and innovation is what distinguishes businesses that are successful from those that merely survive. Examining issues related to creativity and innovation is particularly important in the context of entrepreneurship, because creativity goes far beyond idea generation. The extent that entrepreneurship involves the creation, discovery, evaluation, exploration, and exploitation of opportunities within established private, public, or social sector organizations or as new ventures, creativity and innovation exhibited by individuals, groups, and organizations is a necessity for all entrepreneurial organizations.

References

Amabile, T. M. (1998). How to kill creativity. *Harvard Business Review, 76,* 77–89.

Amabile, T. M. (2004). *Innovation and creativity quotes.* Retrieved July 27, 2004, from www.innovationtools.com/Quotes/Quotes.asp

Brown, B., & Scott, A. D. (2011). How P&G tripled its innovation success rate. *Harvard Business Review, 89*(6), 64–72.

Suggested Readings

Amabile, T. M. (1997). Motivating creativity in organizations: On doing what you love and loving what you do. *California Management Review, 40*(1), 39–58.

The author undertakes two studies at High Tech Electronics International and ascertains that the work environment within an organization is strongly influenced by management at all levels and can make the difference between the production of new, useful ideas for innovative business growth and the continuance of old, progressively less useful routines.

Amabile, T. M., Conti, R., Coon, H., Lazenby, J., & Herron, M. (1996). Assessing the work environment for creativity. *Academy of Management Journal, 39*(5), 1154–1184.

The authors describe the development and validation of a new instrument, KEYS: Assessing the Climate for Creativity, designed to assess perceived stimulants and obstacles to creativity in organizational work environments. Their study shows that perceived work environments, as assessed by the KEYS scales, discriminate between high-creativity projects and low-creativity projects; certain scales discriminate more strongly and consistently than others.

Baron, R. A., & Tang, J. (2011). The role of entrepreneurs in firm-level innovation: Joint effects of positive affect, creativity, and environmental dynamism. *Journal of Business Venturing, 26*(1), 49–60.

In this article, the authors investigate the joint effects, on firm-level innovation, of two variables pertaining to entrepreneurs (their creativity and positive affect) and a key environmental variable (environmental dynamism). Their results show that a positive effect among founding entrepreneurs is significantly related to their creativity and that creativity, in turn, is positively related to firm-level innovation. Both of these relationships are moderated by environmental dynamism, being stronger in highly dynamic than stable environments.

Hirst, G., Van Knippenberg, D., & Zhou, J. (2009). A cross-level perspective on employee creativity: Goal orientation, team learning behavior, and individual creativity. *Academy of Management Journal, 52*(2), 280–293.

In this article, the authors developed and tested a cross-level model of individual creativity, integrating goal orientation theory and team learning research. Their study found cross-level interactions between individuals' goal orientation and team learning behavior in a cross-national sample of 25 R & D teams comprising 198 employees.

Kornish, L. J., & Ulrich, K. T. (2011). Opportunity spaces in innovation: Empirical analysis of large samples of ideas. *Management Science, 57*(1), 107–128.

In this article, the authors analyzed 1,368 ideas from five data sets, each created by different groups of individuals who generated ideas in parallel. Their results found that strict redundancy is not highly prevalent, which suggests that the opportunity spaces are large on the order of thousands of opportunities. Overall, the article suggests identifying themes for clusters can be a useful step in an innovation process, creating a map of the innovation landscape.

CHAPTER 3

Innovation and Entrepreneurship in Context

How does the approach to innovation and entrepreneurship differ between small, medium, and large corporations? What is innovation and entrepreneurship in the context of small and medium enterprises (SMEs) and large corporations? What does the term *open innovation* mean? How can open innovation effectively be pursued? What is the process of innovation? Does this process differ between those pursing radical innovations and those pursuing incremental innovations?

Scenario: Zara Retail

Zara was founded in 1975 by Amancio Ortega. Zara is a brand that is internationally recognized for its high innovation in fashion retail. In 1975, the first Zara store opened in A Coruña, Galicia, Spain, where it is head-quartered today. In 1985, Zara was integrated in a new holding company, Industria de Diseño Textil, S.A. (Inditex). Zara is recognized as the leading chain store of the Inditex group, which owns well-renowned brands such as Massimo Dutti, Pull and Bear, Oysho, Uterqüe, Stradivarius, and Bershka. In 1976, Zara's brand name was positively recognized by the public; this supported the development of additional stores in other Spanish cities.

In December 1988, the first Zara store opened outside Spain in Oporto, Portugal. As a result of their continued success and increasing popularity, Zara started new ventures around the world. In 1989, Zara entered the U.S. market and opened an outlet in New York, and in 1990, it expanded within Europe and opened an outlet in Paris. The Pull and Bear chain was launched in 1991 as well as buying a 65% stake in the Massimo Dutti Group. Inditex continued to enter new international markets including Mexico in 1992, Greece in 1993, and Belgium and Sweden in 1994. In 1995, Inditex acquired the total share of Massimo Dutti. They also opened their first store in Malta in 1995 and in Cyprus in 1996. Norway and Israel were added to their list of countries in 1997.

The Bershka chain, which targeted the younger female market, was launched in 1998, and that same year, stores opened in Argentina, Japan, Kuwait, Lebanon, Turkey, United Arab Emirates, United Kingdom, and Venezuela. With the acquisition of Stradivarius in 1999, it became the group's fifth chain, and it opened more new stores in these countries: Bahrain, Brazil, Canada, Chile, Germany, the Netherlands, Poland, Saudi Arabia, and Uruguay. Stores in Andorra, Austria, Denmark, and Qatar opened in 2000. On May 23, 2001, Inditex went public and was listed on the Spanish stock market. During that same year, the group entered the Czech Republic, Iceland, Ireland, Italy, Jordan, Luxembourg, and Puerto Rico. In 2003, Zara expanded into the home furnishing market and opened its first Zara home store. In 2004, Zara opened its 2,000th store in Hong Kong. Zara franchises the stores when local legislation prevents foreign-owned businesses; otherwise, stores are company owned.

Zara's business model is focused on sustainable development and corporate social responsibility of the society and the environments in which it operates. Zara focuses on saving energy and making their stores eco-friendly. They emphasize waste management; one example of this is that they recycle millions of security tags and hangers each year. Ninety percent of Zara customers carry bags that are made from paper. In the production of certain items of clothing, they support ecological agriculture and use organic cotton. Additionally, they do not use any petroleum derivatives or nonbiodegradable materials in the production of their footwear.

Zara's triumph incorporates numerous styles from formal wear, casual wear, to business clothes. Their business model is totally customer focused, which incorporates the design, production, distribution, and sales through its major retail network. Zara's success is a result of its innovation and the ability to identify and respond to the constant changes in fashion, continuously designing new models that meet and exceed customer needs, wants, and expectations. Zara introduces approximately 11,000 new garments annually. Many lines are replaced within a number of weeks. Zara's business model is flexible to adjust to emerging changes throughout the season, managing them by efficiently and effectively, introducing new products within a short time frame—that is innovation! Producing products within a short time frame is facilitated by local production, advanced information systems that support frequent monitoring and renewal of inventory, and well-accomplished and fast methods of distribution. Zara produces most of its designs in European and North African factories rather than outsourcing to Asia. They closely monitor in-store inventory levels to ensure the correct fit between supply and demand. Each season, models are entirely developed by their creative teams; in 2011, there were over 30,000 models developed. Zara has 200 designers whose designs are inspired by market trends and customer feedback. Capturing the core fashion trends is fundamental for improved margins and higher sales while the item is at full price. By only manufacturing a certain quantity of each style, Zara decreases its exposure to a single product and generates limited editions. By limiting the availability of each style, they are increasing the desirability.

Starting with a single store in 1975, Zara is now in 78 countries and over 1,603 stores centrally positioned in major cities. Its strong international presence demonstrates that there are no barriers to the development of a single fashion culture. Their innovation appears to be very distinctive in relation to competitors in the fashion industry. Zara avoids advertising; seldom has sales; and in an industry where the majority of competitors outsource their manufacturing to less expensive countries, Zara has significant vertical integration, keeping the majority of its production process in-house. These diverse moves are core to its success that gives the company its competitive advantage.

Zara's winning strategy can only exist through innovation. It is technology advancement and development that allows Zara to clearly recognize and manufacture the type of clothes customers want; efficiently bring those products to the market; and remove costs associated with advertising, inventory errors, and sale reductions. A true innovator knows the market as well as the technology, seeks new opportunities with a clear insight of the potential threats as well as strategies to manage these threats. Zara is fully connected to their customers, who contribute to shaping the emerging trends in today's world. This is the key to their success and growth as well as the diversity of people and cultures that are passionate about fashion.

SOURCE: Adapted from www.zara.com, www.Inditex.com, and www.fibre2fashion.com.

Introduction

Innovation and entrepreneurship are a phenomenon that is increasingly important for SMEs and large corporations in all types of industries and sectors in this highly competitive, globalized, fast-changing economy. It is a core feature of society and central to organizational growth and success. It is not just large national and multinational corporations that are innovative and entrepreneurial; there are numerous examples of highly successful innovations from SMEs that have transformed industries. New business start-ups; entrepreneurs; university spin-offs; and small, highly innovative and entrepreneurial organizations frequently produce major innovations. Organizations that are committed to innovation are in a position to take advantage of new markets and opportunities during prosperous economic times and maintain and grow existing business during more challenging ones.

Innovation and entrepreneurship are particularly important in the emergence of the knowledge society and increased globalization in which the generation and commercialization of new knowledge is key for, national, international, and organizational success. It is an important process in the way the generation of knowledge in one organization can be commercialized in another. This has resulted in organizations recognizing the value and importance of what is termed *open innovation.* With open innovation, organizations commercialize internal and external ideas by deploying pathways to the market. Organizations can commercialize internal ideas through channels external to their existing businesses as a way to generate value for the organization. SMEs are an important mechanism for knowledge spillovers when the ideas are generated and abilities, products, processes, strategies, innovations, and technologies are required and commercialized by large national and multinational corporations. SMEs are often the driving force of innovative and entrepreneurial activity and demonstrate technological advancement and development, globalization, and other ways that has changed the significance and process of innovation and technological development.

For SMEs and large corporations to develop innovation and entrepreneurship as part of their strategy and deal with economic challenges, the strategy must be adapted to external environmental conditions. The strategies used by Zara may not work for every organization attempting to be innovative and entrepreneurial; Zara followed its own rules and created its own fashion culture. Having a culture that supports and emphasizes innovation and entrepreneurship with creative thinking *outside the box* is fundamental for national and international development and growth of an organization in a dynamic environment.

In times of economic challenges, organizations need innovation and entrepreneurship more than ever in order to achieve long-term financial sustainability and competitiveness. Organizations cannot stand still but need to be able to adapt to a highly dynamic environment by being innovative and entrepreneurial in ways that respond to the environment and opportunities. While this can be a challenging process, those organizations that can successfully integrate innovation and entrepreneurship as part of the day-to-day organizational philosophy achieve significant benefits.

The objective of this chapter is to examine innovation and entrepreneurship in SMEs and large corporations. Innovation and entrepreneurship are discussed to provide an understanding of their importance for SMEs and large corporations in every industry and sector. The meaning and importance of open innovation and the value it brings to organizations is discussed. Following a discussion on the forms, processes, and sources of innovation, this chapter concludes with a discussion on the importance of innovation as a coupling activity that links the market and technology.

Innovation and Entrepreneurship in Context

Innovation and entrepreneurship are very important as they allow organizations to be competitive and provide them greater resilience in turbulent, uncertain economic environments. During an economic crisis, innovation and entrepreneurship can stimulate the expansion of SMEs and large corporations in their existing or new markets. In the new economy, knowledge has become a primary resource to become more innovative and entrepreneurial. It is fundamental that organizations find new ways of utilizing existing knowledge and creating new knowledge that will stimulate innovation. Through this knowledge, these innovations open the way to new and advanced products and services, new business processes, new management concepts, and new markets. Highly innovative organizations that implement very successful innovation practices include well-known global companies such as 3M, Amazon, Apple, Facebook, Google, Samsung, and Twitter, as well as lesser-known organizations such as Natura (cosmetics), Embraco (international leader in refrigeration), and Petrobras (one of the world's largest energy companies). Building and developing competencies to be entrepreneurial and to innovate new products and services puts the organization in a strong position to meet today's demands and challenges while also being ready to adapt to future environments and circumstances and succeed in tomorrow's innovations. Zara's competitiveness in innovation comes from its drive and determination to consistently produce new things based on customer desires, technological developments, and market changes.

The role of SMEs has changed as competitive advantage has moved closer to knowledge-based economic activity and globalization. SMEs make a significant contribution to the European Union's (EU) economy and are responsible for a significant number of new product innovations, causing large manufacturing corporations to lose competitive advantage. In the EU, 99.8% of enterprises are SMEs; large corporations, account for only 0.2%. EU micro-enterprise performance was most stable in 2009. The recovery in 2010 was spearheaded by SMEs. The SMEs in the EU that are leading the way in innovation are quickly recovering in terms of value add compared to their counterparts that are modest innovators. In 2009, the United States had a larger reduction in SME employment (-6.0%) in comparison to the EU (-2.7%). Prior to the European recession, there was a downward trend in SME development in Japan.

Economic downturns frequently generate a growth in the number of business start-ups. However, in the United States there was a fall in the number of SMEs in 2009 whereas the number of large enterprises marginally increased. The potential for innovation and entrepreneurship in SMEs and large corporations has been challenged by the global recession. Organizations in all industries and sectors need to manage this through knowledge and the development of external relationships. This requires organizations to develop and implement better approaches to innovation and entrepreneurial strategies in order to not just survive but to achieve a competitive, sustainable position no matter what economic environment they may encounter.

Open Innovation

Innovation and entrepreneurship are major factors for organizations in achieving economic success and sustainability. In today's challenging, dynamic, and competitive global market, organizations need to be innovative and entrepreneurial and create commercially viable, high quality products and services more efficiently and effectively than before. To address these challenges, organizations need to develop new techniques to the strategies and processes of their innovations that will give them every opportunity to achieve their full potential and to be the best they can in light of economic conditions.

Organizations are now facing intensified global competitiveness and increasing research and development (R & D) expenditures. Their own R & D efforts are no longer sufficient for their survival and sustainability but need to develop and implement new approaches to innovation in order to achieve competitiveness. Open innovation, a term developed by Henry Chesbrough, is one key approach that organizations are embracing. As originally defined by Henry Chesbrough (2003), open innovation is a paradigm that assumes that firms can and should use external ideas, as well as internal ideas, and internal and external paths to the market as the firms look to advance their technology. Open innovation combines internal and external ideas into architectures and systems whose requirements are defined by a business model (Chesbrough, 2003). It refers to the collaborative methods applied and may imply the payment of license fees between organizations for intellectual property. Open innovation is the internal and external flow of knowledge to drive innovation within an organization and develop the markets to externally utilize the innovation.

Increasingly, innovation concentrates on knowledge beyond the organizational boundaries. This highlights the importance of organizations using external as well as internal ideas as they look to develop their innovations. Organizations need to recognize that since knowledge is widely distributed, they cannot just depend on their own R & D. Instead, they need to acquire inventions or intellectual property from other organizations when it advances and develops their business model. The transition from internal R & D to external connection and development creates opportunities for all organizations in all industries and sectors to go beyond their core competencies and remain competitive in an increasingly complex, uncertain, and changing environment.

Open innovation is an important network for organizations to extend their opportunities for new innovations and technological advancement through collaboration with partners such as suppliers, customers, or universities as a way to develop and commercialize the most innovative products or services ahead of competitors. For example, IBM collaborates with academic colleagues; the objective is efficiently and effectively responding to the fast-changing world. The Alcatel-Lucent Community of Open Innovation and Research enables Bell Labs researchers to work with external partners on mutually beneficial research projects. Alcatel-Lucent has researchers and technologists around the world focused on open innovation, exploration, and discovery so they can achieve success and competitiveness in terms of best products, services, and solutions. Xerox extended their own capabilities by collaborating with organizations worldwide. This internationally collaborative knowledge resource enhances the organization's competencies and develops products and solutions that meet the market requirements. At Xerox, open innovation partnerships include university-sponsored projects and collaborations with customers and other corporations.

Large corporations have transferred R & D activities internationally to their global value chain and depend on external innovation for new products, services, and processes. Procter & Gamble (P&G) is a good example of an organization that uses open innovation to develop products and drive growth. P&G seeks ideas in 85 different networks and more than 120 universities. With 75% of the searches resulting in "viable leads," their website is in five languages to encourage unsolicited submissions, and over 50% of their innovation is externally sourced. Through P&G's Connect + Develop program, they seek ideas for almost every part of their operations such as new products, technological developments, business model, packaging or design, or ideas for developing existing P&G products. Nokia Research Center engages in open innovation through research partnerships with internationally renowned institutions. These collaborations increase the efficiency and effectiveness of their innovations and generate greater value for the organizations and customers. 3M's ability to keep churning out new innovations is very much dependent on the organization's long-standing commitment to open innovation.

The core value of open innovation to organizations is that it utilizes resources and generates more ideas. Open innovation creates close collaboration between the organization and external partners—customers, suppliers, universities, or other people. The objective for collaboration between organizations is to take advantage of new business opportunities, to share risks, and to generate synergy through partnering complementary resources. Open innovation is a strategic pursuit that allows organizations in all industries and sectors to identify lower risk and novel growth opportunities. Large corporations are more likely to develop open innovation partnerships than SMEs. SMEs can participate sooner, move faster, and more readily adapt to opportunities that emerge from the periphery of a market in comparison to large corporations (Chesbrough, 2010). There are many opportunities for SMEs in the world of open innovation. They can pursue smaller markets or expand into larger developing markets—particularly when investment in R & D is not exorbitant and their business strategy is highly innovative. They can collaborate with leading businesses and platforms of large corporations. SMEs can have a different position than large corporations in the same industry. For example, Budweiser, Coors, Heineken, and Miller are key players in the brewing industry, while numerous microbreweries hold different niche positions. There are many challenges for SMEs in their attempt to compete in markets with large corporations. SMEs that are alert, adaptive, and focused have the potential to do well and take advantage of their uniqueness over large corporations. Large corporations would benefit from working more closely with SMEs. SMEs are potential suppliers, partners, or customers for large corporations.

To meet the increasing demand for innovation from customers, suppliers, and society at large with the worldwide advancement of science and technology, organizations (predominately large corporations) increasingly incorporate innovation *ecosystems* internationally. These innovation networks allow organizations to collaborate with individuals, institutions (universities, government agencies), and other worldwide organizations to resolve problems and develop new ideas. In the current global climate, innovation is more and more significant for organizations to actively engage in both external and intrafirm networks. The drive for global open innovation is strongly influenced by the technological and industrial context in which the organization operates. The model of open innovation is more prevalent in the information and communication technology (ICT) and pharmaceuticals-biotechnology sectors and is also becoming important in the automotive and aerospace industries.

As anticipated by Drucker (1995), knowledge has become the key economic resource and the dominant source of competitive advantage today. Therefore, open innovation needs to be ingrained in the overall organizational strategy that clearly recognizes external ideas, knowledge, technology, and market factors in creating value. This can create significant value for the organization in whatever form of innovation they aim to achieve.

Forms of Innovation

Innovation can take many forms, such as developing new products and services, developing new methods of production, identifying new sources of supply, identifying new markets, and developing new organizational strategies. As discussed in Chapter 2, innovations can be breakthrough, technological, or incremental and can vary in their degrees of uniqueness. Most innovations introduced to the market are incremental innovations, which have limited uniqueness or technological advancement. There are less breakthrough innovations and technological innovations. Regardless of the degree of uniqueness or technological advancement, each innovation—most significantly breakthrough and technological innovations—evolve and develop into commercialized products/services that create value and generate economic wealth.

Breakthrough innovation—also known as radical innovation—represents the invention of something new, significantly changing customer expectations in a positive way. Radical innovations have a significant impact on the market by providing new customer benefits in relation to existing product generation within the category and the organization in terms of its ability to create new business venturing. It carries with it the greatest level of risk, highest cost, and longest time scale for development. Recent examples include the technological breakthrough in social networking with the launch of Facebook. Amazon's Internet-based approach to selling books allowed them to offer many more books than any bookstore. This resulted in a number of bookstores going out of business. As of 2010, Amazon was the largest online retailer in the United States. Transistors developed by Bell Labs uprooted the major players in the electronics industry who were concentrating on vacuum tube technology.

Technological innovation represents the application of existing science and technology. It is a dramatic improvement on existing innovations, but is not subjected to the same degree of risk or uncertainty. The time scales involved in the introduction of innovations are shorter in comparison to breakthrough innovations. Computers and their components, cellular phones, smart phones, iPhones, digital cameras and memory cards, iPods, iPads, iPad minis, and MP5 players are all examples of technological innovations.

Incremental innovation is the form of innovation that occurs most frequently. This level of innovation represents the adaptation of existing technologies and products with a different and generally enhanced market appeal. It is the fine-tuning of what already exists. It is the easiest form of innovation to offer—along with being the cheapest and least vulnerable to failure. Incremental improvements are evident with the Apple iPod, which is now available in many different colors and can store photographs and videos. Intel's incremental improvement includes the modification of the Pentium 3 chip with the introduction of the Pentium 4 computer processor chip. The modification included improvements to the design and more features to enhance the overall performance of the chip. Incremental improvements have occurred over time to automobiles, which now are all expected to include electric windows and mirrors, ABS brakes, air bags, and so forth. Consumers expect organizations in all sectors and industries to make at least incremental improvements to existing products and services. Making incremental improvements is fundamental for extending the market life of a product or service.

The actual form of innovation that an organization is pursuing has a significant impact on the actual innovation process. Organizations that pursue breakthrough innovations require a very different level of creativity and R & D compared to those that are undertaking incremental innovations. SMEs and large corporations in all industries and sectors need to focus on the type of innovations they are pursuing and take the appropriate course of action in their development and commercialization. Breakthrough innovations and technological innovations require a significant level of creativity and a more in-depth diverse level of R & D in order to invent something new that will be commercially viable and create value in comparison to incremental innovations that focus on existing innovations. Successful organizations pursuing breakthrough and technological innovations are now going beyond their organizational boundaries in recognition of the need to deeply engage in invention and development of new knowledge.

Whether innovation is breakthrough, technological, or incremental, it is accelerated by globalization, economic conditions, and the pace of change within the industry. In order to remain competitive and achieve success in terms of growth and development, the pace of change inside the organization must be greater than the company's external changes. Innovation is the key success factor (KSF) in most industries and sectors to achieve sustained growth and profitability and improve the quality of life in society. Successful organizations that are characterized by being innovative are focused, flexible, and fast; they seek opportunities through open innovation, synergy, alliances, and venturing. Zara takes, on average, 15 days for a concept to go from idea generation to being available in a store. Most of the in-store products in Zara did not exist 3 weeks earlier, making them more flexible and adaptable to the market in comparison to competitors such as Gap and H&M. Organizations that fail to innovate particularly in uncertain and turbulent environments are putting their business at risk.

Sources of Innovation

Innovation generated by the creative acts of organizational members cannot be predicted. Innovation is not a rational activity as it depends on the creative acts of individual members, and these cannot be anticipated or programmed. Innovative organizations can, however, develop an organizational context that motivates and generates creativity and supports the innovation process. Individuals and teams are a key source of innovation in all areas and at all levels of the organization, but they must be supported and facilitated in their innovative endeavors. R & D enables organizations to access a broad set of external sources of knowledge in pursuit of innovations. Open innovation extends opportunities for innovation beyond the organizational boundaries and generates collaborations with suppliers, customers, universities, and research institutes.

Opportunities for Innovation

Before the process of innovation can result in meaningful results, organizations must have a general idea about the desired innovation. There are formal and informal approaches for identifying opportunities for innovation. Although formal approaches are generally found within more established large corporations seeking breakthrough and technological innovations with a strong R & D team, most organizations use informal sources for incremental innovations, such as being responsive to the complaints and comments of customer, suppliers, and the wider community. While there are many sources of innovation, it is important that each organization uses every source available in their search for breakthrough, technological, or incremental innovative opportunities. These sources provide both internal and external opportunities.

Internal organizational opportunities to innovate include the following:

- Product innovation—development of new products, changes in design of existing products, or use of new materials or components in manufacturing existing products.
- New distribution channels and routes to market—they broaden customer base and can extend market share.
- New approaches to selling and promotion—ties to the customers' needs and provides opportunities to improve competitiveness. It is critical to understand the buying process, decision process, and key influencers and to know what competitors are doing.
- Customer servicing innovation—being more customer-focused as only satisfied customers will give return business. The key to achieving service innovation is listening to customers, understanding their service needs and working to exceed customer needs.
- Reinventing operations or manufacturing—optimizing processes to have greater efficiency and effectiveness in manufacturing and delivery. Optimizing processes makes it easier for customers to do business with the organization and reduces costs.
- Improving profitability, growth, and development—successful innovations enhance organizational profitability and generate opportunities for future growth and development. The key is to understand what products, services, or areas contribute to real profitability.
- Restructuring the business to become more innovative and responsive to market conditions—this can be a very dramatic source of innovation. It can involve acquisitions, joint venture, divestments, alliances, and financial restructuring.

External organizational opportunities to innovate include the following:

- Reinventing the business system—redeveloping the system to meet the market demands and customer needs with the objective of increasing market share and competitiveness.
- Changing/innovating in market positioning—being adaptable and flexible to seek opportunities that position the organization more innovatively within the market. The key to growth in most markets necessitates being able to segment and resegment markets. Comprehensive knowledge of customers and competitors is fundamental.

The Process of Innovation

An innovation may not be entirely new or unfamiliar to an organization, but it should involve some identifiable change. Innovation is the effort to create purposeful, focused change in the economic and social environment. Founders of innovative new ventures such as Anita Roddick (Body Shop), Herb Kelleher (Southwest Airlines), Pierre Omidyar (eBay), Jeff Bezos (Amazon), Niklas Zennström (Skype), Michael Dell (Dell Computer), Bill Gates (Microsoft), Richard Branson (Virgin Group), and Mark Zuckerberg (Facebook) are highly innovative entrepreneurs in comparison to entrepreneurs who establish less innovative ventures such as a McDonald's franchise, Subway franchise, a Mercedes-Benz dealership, a newsstand, or a consulting business.

The innovation process is more than creating a good idea. The role of creative thinking is fundamental to its development. Innovation is a dynamic process involving both structural and social conditions. The sequence of steps in the innovation process typically starts with the awareness of a need and ends with the implementation of an innovation to satisfy the need. The level and depth of analysis at each stage of the process is dependent on the type of innovation and the organizational resources.

A breakthrough or technological innovation is usually more labor intensive, time consuming, and costly as it requires the invention of new knowledge in the case of breakthrough innovation or the innovative extension and development of an existing innovation in the case of technological innovation. Whereas incremental innovation is much more focused on the improvements to existing innovations, this is important for an organization to retain this market position. Large corporations have more resources to develop R & D than SMEs. Open innovation is one way for SMEs to extend and develop their ability to engage in the development of more high potential forms of innovation.

Steps in the Innovation Process

- Generating ideas and recognizing opportunities
- Analyzing the relevant areas and facts
- Developing insights based on the analysis
- Seeking connections or bridging
- Seeking creative leaps
- Developing concepts
- Evaluating alternatives
- Selecting and planning for implementation
- Carrying out Implementation

> The creative search for radical, technological, or incremental innovation, or new possibilities for innovation

Once the *opportunity* is recognized, the evaluation process commences. It is important to understand the factors that create the opportunity: technology, market changes, competition, or changes in government regulations. This creates the knowledge base for the innovation. At this stage, it is important for an organization to look outside the status quo; it is beneficial to include advisors or other outside individuals who are not involved in the day-to-day operations of the organization. The *analysis* must be completed in all the activity areas associated with the idea. This involves gathering and understanding all the data. It is important that the idea fit the personal skills and goals of the organization. In the process of evaluating an opportunity, the necessary resources should be clearly defined and obtained at a low cost. The organization must *develop insights* into new ways for looking at the business based on the completed analysis and implications of trends and expected changes, develop scenarios and examine implications, identify the key issues to be addressed, evaluate potential shortcomings vis-à-vis the KSFs, and reverse roles and step in the shoes of the competitor or customer to gain a greater insight. Once insights are gained, the organization needs to *seek connections* to fill the existing gap in the market and find novel combinations of products, services, processes, and packaging. This requires looking beyond the industry for fresh ideas that could be imported. This leads to *creative leaps,* enabling the organization to creatively think about what would be ideal within the industry that would generate more profit, lead to competitive advantage, and become a market leader. Once the ideal is determined, they can compare their current knowledge and identify the gaps. Through research, a broad range of unknowns can be mastered, including emerging technologies, societal change, and customer values and in the process identify major opportunities for innovation.

The next stage is *developing concepts,* which is a difficult but high value-added stage because lots of ideas have been generated and now some need to create potentially viable business propositions. This is a time consuming stage, but organizations must not rush this as it will cost in the long term.

The *evaluating alternatives* stage requires an organized process to prioritize and choose from the concepts developed. There is still the opportunity to improve concepts at this stage. The best alternative is the one that fits the overall goals and values of the organization and achieves the desired innovation results.

The *selecting and planning for implementation* stage requires an in-depth evaluation to ensure that it is commercially viable and will create value. This is required because the ultimate success of the selected innovation is whether it can be translated into action.

The final stage—*implementation*—involves the abilities of the organization and its team to ensure that the chosen innovation is carried out effectively. Once implemented, the innovation must be evaluated to identify any deviations on whether it can be understood and supported by the internal organization.

Innovation, Technology, and Market Factors

Technology and market factors are significant in stimulating innovation. Innovation has been characterized by a coupling of technology and the market (Rothwell, 1992). Successful innovations involve a creative coupling of technological and market factors because no organization works in isolation of technological advancements and development and market conditions (see Figure 3.1). Organizations need to develop their innovations that will add to the existing technological and market factors; otherwise, they risk failure. The key challenge that organizations have to manage with any invention and innovation is that technology and markets are constantly changing; organizations need to be flexible and adaptable to those changes. Technological changes are at such a fast pace that what is technically unachievable today may be feasible in a few years' time due to scientific advancements. Likewise, goods that are not sold in the market today may become a necessity by tomorrow's consumers.

The relationship between the development of innovation, technology, and market factors is complex, particularly with today's technological

Figure 3.1 Innovation as a Coupling Activity Linking Technology and Market Factors

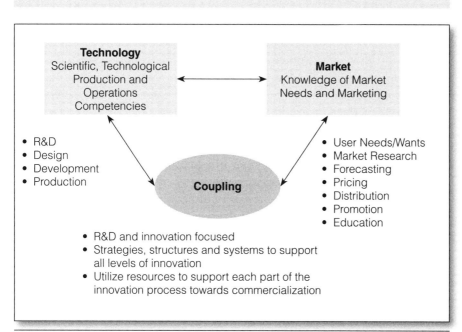

SOURCE: Adapted from Rothwell, R. (1992). Successful industrial innovation: Critical factors for the 1990s. R&D *Management, 22*(3), 221–240.

advancements and fast-changing markets. The competencies of the organizations and the individuals operating at the interfaces between these areas connect technological and market opportunities. This "coupling" activity is evident in Zara as it is technology that helps them identify and manufacture clothes that meet the specification of customers and get the products to the market efficiently and effectively. Organizations need to scan the market and the state-of-the-art technology in search of new, competitive opportunities. The coupling between technology and market needs is important at every stage of the innovation process from the idea generation through the entire research, design, and development process to the introduction of the new product or process into the marketplace.

Summary

Innovation and entrepreneurship are a KSF in large corporations and SMEs in virtually all industries and sectors. The main sources of innovation are individuals and teams working within the organization in cooperation with key participants within the external environment including suppliers, customers, and universities. There are many areas of opportunity for innovations in organizations. Organizations need to use their resources in order to identify every potential opportunity for innovation and take appropriate action to develop and implement innovations that will create value and give them a competitive edge. The steps in the innovation process are all well known, but the most important ones are those associated with the creative search for new solutions and new possibilities that will take the organization into the future.

The key challenge facing organizations is being able to build a congruent innovative organization and have the commitment, drive, and know-how to continue to develop the innovation in the future. Both large corporations and SMEs need to be organized to build internal diversity and external collaborations through the open innovation process. For organizations to develop and grow in dynamic, uncertain environments, they need to "couple" the internal innovations with technological and market factors. Truly successful innovations are those that not just meet but exceed the needs of the market.

References

Chesbrough, H. (2003). *Open innovation: The new imperative for creating and profiting from technology.* Boston: Harvard Business Press.

Chesbrough, H. (2010). Open innovation: A key to achieving socioeconomic evolution. How smaller companies can benefit from open innovation. *Economy, Culture, and History: Japan Spotlight Bimonthly: JAPECO,* 169.

Drucker, P. (1995). *Managing in time of great change.* New York: Truman Talley Books.

Rothwell, R. (1992). Successful industrial innovation: Critical factors for the 1990s. *R&D Management, 22*(3), 221–240.

Suggested Readings

Chesbrough, H. (2012). GE's ecomagination Challenge: An experiment in open innovation. *California Management Review,* 54(3), 140–154.

In this article, the author provides a case study of GE's ecomagination Challenge. The ecomagination Challenge has led to a number of new start-ups being funded, but from GE's perspective, the hard work was just starting. In order for the ecomagination Challenge to pay off for GE, some of the nascent ventures would need to gain scale or accelerate the growth of an existing GE business.

Kickul, J. R., Griffiths, M. D., Jayaram, J., & Wagner, S. M. (2011). Operations management, entrepreneurship, and value creation: Emerging opportunities in a cross-disciplinary context. *Journal of Operations Management, 29*(1–2), 78–85.

The authors discuss five articles in the special issue and conclude that the intersection of entrepreneurship and operations management is about value creation. They assert that the innovative entrepreneur has the vision of a new product, service, or method of production or delivery. Operations management provides the best practices for the entrepreneur to reach his/her goal within the environment while recognizing the opportunities and constraints that exist. Overall they conclude that cooperation between entrepreneurship and operations management should result in fewer failures and greater successes.

Lasagni, A. (2012). How can external relationships enhance innovation in SMEs? New evidence for Europe. *Journal of Small Business Management, 50*(2), 310–339.

In this article, the author investigates the role of external relationships as key drivers of small business innovation. The empirical analysis is based on data for approximately 500 SMEs in six European countries. The results indicate that innovation performance is higher in SMEs that are proactive in strengthening their relationships with innovative suppliers, users, and customers. Additionally, the findings support the view that SMEs will have better new product development results if they improve their relationships with laboratories and research institutes.

Lichtenthaler, U. (2011). Open innovation: Past research, current debates, and future directions. *Academy of Management Perspectives, 25*(1), 75–93.

The authors in this article evaluate the literature on open innovation and assess whether open is a sustainable trend rather than a management fashion. They develop a conceptual framework that provides the foundation for discussing open innovation processes and their implications for managing open innovation at the organizational, project, and individual level.

Nieto, M. J., & Santamaría, L. (2010). Technological collaboration: Bridging the innovation gap between small and large firms. *Journal of Small Business Management, 48*(1), 44–69.

In this article, the authors analyze how technological collaboration acts as an input to the innovation process and allows SMEs to bridge the innovation gap with their bigger counterparts. Based on a large longitudinal sample of Spanish manufacturing firms, the results show that though technological collaboration is a useful mechanism for firms of all sizes to improve innovativeness, it is a critical factor for the smallest firms.

Oke, A., & Idiagbon-Oke, M. (2010). Communication channels, innovation tasks and NPD project outcomes in innovation-driven horizontal networks. *Journal of Operations Management, 28*(5), 442–453.

In this study, the authors investigate the link between the innovation task analyzability and the richness of communications channels used in network arrangements and the link between task analyzability and ties and project development time. The results found a negative link from task analyzability to communication channel richness and a positive link from communication channel richness to ties.

Parida, V., Westerberg, M., & Frishammar, J. (2012). Inbound open innovation activities in high-tech SMEs: The impact on innovation performance. *Journal of Small Business Management, 50*(2), 283–309.

In this article, the authors investigate the effects of four inbound open innovation activities on innovation performance of SMEs. Their results found that different open innovation activities are beneficial for different innovation outcomes. For instance, technology sourcing is linked to radical innovation performance whereas technology scouting is linked to incremental innovation performance.

SECTION 2

MANAGING INNOVATION AND ENTREPRENEURSHIP

CHAPTER 4

Building an Innovative and Entrepreneurial Organization

What impact does the changing environment have on innovation and entrepreneurship within an organization? What is the role of strategic management in the development of an innovative and entrepreneurial organization? What is the link between innovation and entrepreneurship with strategy, and how can this be developed? What internal organizational characteristics make some organizations more innovative and entrepreneurial than others?

Scenario: Xerox

Founded in 1903, the M.H. Kuhn Company became the Haloid Company in 1906 in Rochester, New York, with the focus of manufacturing and selling photographic paper. Chester Carlson (American inventor, physicist, and patent attorney) was the man whose discovery of xerographic printing fueled Xerox's global growth and changed an industry. Carlson pursued the concept of electrophotography and in 1938 made the first xerographic image—a handwritten notation of "10-22-38 ASTORIA"—in his Astoria, Queens, New York City lab. In 1948, xerography was formally announced, and that same year the word *Xerox* was trademarked. In 1949, based on the process outlined in Carlson's xerography manual, the Model A became the world's first xerographic copier, requiring multiple steps to produce a single copy. The Haloid Company and the Rank

Organization plc (United Kingdom) formed Rank Xerox in 1956 as a joint venture to manufacture and market Haloid (later Xerox) equipment initially in Europe and eventually in Africa and Asia. In 1958, the Haloid Company changed its name to Haloid Xerox Inc. to reflect the organization's focus on commercial xerography. Further emphasizing their focus on xerographic products and services, in 1961 Haloid Xerox Inc. changed its name to Xerox Corporation.

In 1962, Rank Xerox Limited and Fuji Photo Film Co. Ltd., a Japanese photographic firm, formed a joint venture known as Fuji Xerox Co. Ltd. to distribute Rank Xerox products later to undertake significant research and development (R & D). In 1970, the Palo Alto Research Center, known as Xerox PARC, opened in Palo Alto, California. This world-class team of experts in information and physical sciences was formed to create "The Office of the Future." Their innovative strategy, leadership, and focus on R & D were developing further. R & D has been the foundation of growth for Xerox.

The Xerox Research Centre of Canada (XRCC) was established in 1974 as an exploratory chemistry research center for Xerox Corporation in Mississauga, Ontario; this became fundamental to their worldwide research operations. Xerox's total quality process, Leadership through Quality, was announced in 1983, leading the organizational quest for business excellence and customer satisfaction. In 1986, Xerox anticipated the major growth and utility of the Internet and registered www.xerox.com, the seventh dot-com top-level domain name to be registered with the Department of Defense.

In 1988, fifty years after Chester Carlson produced the first xerographic image, the 50 Series copiers were launched to recognize his game-changing achievement. Also that year, Xerox produced its 2-millionth copier. This emphasized their worldwide market presence, history of innovation, and commitment to customer success. In 1989, Xerox formed a joint venture with a division of Soviet State Publishing; this was the first public copy center for the Soviet Union. In 1990, they announced the Total Satisfaction Guarantee, which emphasized their dedication to customer success through ultimate quality in design, manufacture, and service of all products sold. Xerox and Fuji Xerox formed Xerox International Partners in 1991. Xerox announced a partnership with Microsoft in 1993 to combine Microsoft at Work architecture with advanced Xerox document imaging technologies in a new family of fax machines, printers, and digital copiers.

In 1997, Xerox purchased the Rank Organization's remaining interest in Rank Xerox and renamed the unit Xerox Europe. Xerox partnered with IBM in 1998 to connect IBM's Lotus Notes and Domino electronic document management environment with the Xerox Document Centre family. Xerox purchased the remaining interest in the partnership between Xerox Corporation (United States) and the Rank Organization (United Kingdom) in 1999, which was renamed Xerox Limited. In 2002, PARC was incorporated as a wholly owned Xerox research company, which still provides important technology to product offerings.

The iGen3 Digital Production Press, which was launched in 2002, developed a receptive global digital printing market in 2003 when Xerox delivered their 100th system. By 2004, it was installed worldwide. Xerox joined Microsoft and other companies as sponsors of the Information Work Productivity Center at MIT in 2003, forming an effort to study how organizations can use technology to increase productivity. The 10,000th installation of the DocuColor 2000 Series press occurred in 2004. This was a significant accomplishment in digital production color printing. Tapping a $20 billion market opportunity, in 2005, Xerox signed consulting and document management contracts with global companies in a number of industries including chemical, automotive, entertainment, security, technology, and financial.

In addition to their business solutions portfolio, in 2006 Xerox acquired XMPie, a leading provider of variable information software. Their $1.5 billion acquisition of Global Imaging Systems in 2007 pairs its small and medium enterprise (SME) market expertise and nationwide distribution network with rapidly expanding document product and service portfolio. Their purchase of Affiliated Computer Services (ACS), the world's largest diversified business process outsourcing (BPO) organization in 2010, led them to become a $22 billion global leader in business process and document management. This purchase gave Xerox access to new business and government clients, and advanced technologies.

Xerox is a global leader in document technology and services. Acquisitions play a key role in their entrepreneurship and innovation model, giving Xerox access to new customers and markets. The Xerox Innovation Group has a balanced portfolio of research and technology projects that focus on today's business requirements as well as identifying and creating future opportunities. Their project focus is short, medium, and long term, and for each project, they undertake the role of partners, incubators, or explorers. Approximately 35% of their research investments support business partners. Researchers closely collaborate with development engineers to quickly take advantage of opportunities for new technologies and services. Another 35% of research investments are focused on the creation of next generation technologies and services or to incubate new offering concepts. The remaining 30% of research investment explore future opportunities and build and develop insight into the potential of new technologies.

Innovation at Xerox covers a wide spectrum of businesses and includes a number of disciplines and competencies. Their goal is to create value for customers, shareholders, and individuals by aligning investments and positively influencing the future in core designated areas. Xerox strongly focuses on creating the most conducive environment for creativity and innovation. Xerox research is where creativity and entrepreneurship are valued and leadership encourages and motivates people to achieve results. They have created an inclusive organizational environment where individuals from a wide range of disciplines and cultures flourish. Additionally, they leverage an ecosystem of the best ideas, technologies, and capabilities from Open Innovation partners.

Innovation continues to flourish at Xerox and the culture encourages creative thinking, where their people are challenged to consider how the idea fits into the overall value chain. There are 140,000 employees in 160 countries in 2012. The company allocated 3.2% of revenue to R & D. In 2010, they invested $1.6 billion in R & D and engineering. Xerox has R & D centers in the United States, Canada, and, Europe and an Innovation Hub in India. The company has 10,700 active patents indicating their dedication and commitment to innovation. They have developed strong open innovation partnerships. The most significant partnership is their joint-venture partner Fuji Xerox in Japan, which was established in 1962. They are clearly a highly creative and innovative organization that leads the way in R & D.

SOURCE: Adapted from www.xerox.com.

Introduction

SMEs and large corporations need to be innovative and entrepreneurial if they are to survive, develop, and grow today and in the future. The environment is now driven by a rapid pace of technological change, increased global competition, and the advancement and development of a knowledge-based economy. Market and product demands are continuously changing. Customers are now demanding more choices and options, product life cycles are shorter, market boundaries are vague, and there is increased global competitiveness. Due to the heightened impact of the fast-changing environment, organizations need to be flexible and adaptable to take advantage of and capitalize on any window of opportunity that emerges, introduce new products, develop new versions of existing products, and efficiently and effectively respond to market changes as well as envisage future market changes.

Innovation and entrepreneurship are a core part of organizations today and are an integral component of the organization's strategy. Strategy aims to capture where the organization wants to go and how it plans to get there. While every situation is different and there is no universal strategy that can be applied to companies, it is important that companies evaluate their own circumstances and market in order to find the best way to be competitive and have a sustainable competitive advantage. The core essence of strategy is being unique. Companies such as IKEA, Southwest Airlines, and Walmart have developed strategies that are unique, internally consistent, and difficult to copy, which has generated sustained competitive advantage.

Strategy is the relationship or fit between the organization and its environment. The integration of innovation and entrepreneurship with strategy enhances the organization's success and value.

To facilitate the integration of innovation and entrepreneurship with strategy, organizations need to implement a strategy that focuses on such key areas as top management support, longer time horizons, flexible organizational structures, and a culture that is conducive to innovation and entrepreneurship. The movement toward a more participative, less hostile culture will fail if it is not supported by appropriate strategy that incorporates innovation and entrepreneurship. The integration of innovation and entrepreneurship implies that value creation plays a key role in the strategic direction of an organization. In all innovative and entrepreneurial endeavors, organizations need to keep focused on customers and stakeholders. Xerox enhances market relevance of all their research on what they call "Customer Led Innovation" where researchers work directly with customers to fully understand their needs and respond to their concerns.

This chapter examines the integration of innovation and entrepreneurship with strategy. Factors within the changing environment that generate the need for this integration will be discussed. The roles of innovation, entrepreneurship, and strategy in achieving sustainable competitive advantage are reviewed along with their integration to enhance competitiveness and value creation for the organization. This chapter discusses the nature of top management support, structure, systems, and culture in building and sustaining innovation and entrepreneurship within the organization. The chapter concludes with a discussion on the need for the integration between innovation and entrepreneurship with strategy to be customer focused in that it meets and exceeds the unmet needs of customers and potential customers.

The Changing Environment

Organizations are now operating in a highly competitive environment that can be characterized in terms of increasing risk, limited ability to forecast, fluid organizational and industry boundaries, new structures and systems that permit and create change, and more diverse customer demands and expectations. No organization is isolated from the external environment, and there is continuous pressure to adapt and change if they are to survive and grow. The external environment includes everything outside the organization, including the political, economic, social, technological, regulatory, competitive, supplier, and customer environments. The level and pace of change is significantly greater than ever before, which has important implications for organizations and how they are managed. Collectively, changes in the environment create important consequences for the development and management of products, markets, and organizational capabilities. As external environments become more complex, dynamic, and turbulent, it also means that there are alternative opportunities. The rapid pace of change is emerging from new markets, technologies, economic conditions, demographic patterns, globalization, and the knowledge economy. Organizations now need to be more innovative than ever. While these changes eliminate some innovations and entrepreneurial activities, they open up opportunities for others. New markets mean new opportunities, and new technologies create new competencies. Some organizations aim to protect themselves against external threats and changing conditions. Others embrace the potential opportunities that can be found as a result of the threat.

In today's environment, to sustain competitive advantage, organizations need to recognize that customer groupings are more differentiated and competition has intensified. Change in one area such as technological advancement and development has resulted in changes in other areas such as more intensified competition as customers have access to a much broader and diverse group of companies to buy goods. For example, originally Google was a search engine; currently it has the world's leading mobile platform in Android and provides a strong alternative to Facebook in Google+. Amazon originally sold books; now it sells services competing with Apple iOS devices and Android. Apple originally sold computers and MP3 players; now it sells phones and tablets, dominating the market with the iPhone and the launch of the iPhone 4S, which introduced a new approach to search technology with Siri, its voice-activated search and task-completion service built in. Apple's iPhone 4S Siri voice search has intensified competition for Google. More recently, Apple launched the iPhone 5 and iPad mini, which emphasizes the significant pace of innovation necessary in the technology industry to stay competitive. Facebook provided the most disruptive web platform since Google's search engine. With 1.06 billion active users and growing, Facebook is rapidly extending its tendrils into the web at large; this competes with Android, Apple, and Google. To be successful, organizations must continually reduce costs, improve quality, enhance customer service, exceed customer expectations, and offer products and services that are innovative and have what customers value. These improvements are the very basic requirement to retain some market share.

Being competitive is very different than achieving sustainable competitive advantage. Achieving competitive advantage needs to be a core part of strategy and instilled within the management philosophy so that the organization will continually be innovative and entrepreneurial and this strategy is the foundation of the organizational culture. Competitive advantage requires organizations to do the following:

- Adapt to external environmental changes
- Be customer driven and focused
- Have flexible strategies and processes that can meet the needs and diverse requirements of customers, suppliers, distributors, regulators, and stakeholders
- Be able to quickly respond to the fast pace of change in the environment by recognizing and taking advantage of opportunities that emerge
- Proactively meet and exceed the needs of customers in light of existing competition
- Actively engage in R & D to continuously prioritize the development of new products, services, processes, markets, and technologies

Organizations that are more adaptable, focused, flexible, responsive, proactive, and engaged in R & D are in a more favorable position not only to adapt to the complex, dynamic external environment but to generate change within that environment and sustain competiveness. Innovation and entrepreneurship are the key sources of sustainable competitive advantage as evident from leading entrepreneurs such as Richard Branson (Virgin Group), Bill Gates (Microsoft), Pierre Omidyar (eBay), and Mark Zuckerberg (Facebook). Continuous innovation, entrepreneurial activity, and an ability to bring about positive changes are the key success factors (KSFs) that define corporate performance in the dynamic, complex, knowledge economy of the 21st century.

The Role of Innovation, Entrepreneurship, and Strategy in Achieving Sustainable Competitive Advantage

Innovative and entrepreneurial organizations develop a strategy that can effectively lead to the commercialization of the new and novel products or services in the marketplace with a sustainable competitive advantage. Strategic management and entrepreneurship are dynamic processes that are intended to enhance organizational performance (Kuratko & Audretsch, 2009).

Strategic management focuses on how competitive positioning can create advantages for organizations that, in turn, enhance performance (Porter, 1980, 1996) and achieve sustained competitive advantage. Strategic planning requires top management to focus beyond the current external environment and envisage the organization's market position in the short, medium, and long term. It necessitates the ability to evaluate the resources and core competencies in terms of how they can be utilized to create new sources of value.

Innovation and entrepreneurship are the key to successfully developing competitive advantages. The challenge is to develop innovation and entrepreneurship as a core competence of the organization. In a global competitive economy, the most successful strategies are those that are integrated with innovative and entrepreneurial activities that offer superior value and create wealth. Strategy and strategic management define the direction of the organization and how well it is achieved. Management needs to develop a strategy that focuses on the best ways for the organization to create and sustain a competitive advantage while simultaneously identifying and developing new opportunities. Innovation and entrepreneurship are focused on searching for new opportunities that will create value for the organization, customers, and stakeholders. Strategy is focused on sustaining competitive advantage and achieving above-average returns. Simultaneously embracing entrepreneurial philosophies, an entrepreneurial climate, and entrepreneurial strategic behaviors increases the likelihood an organization will identify and use its unique capabilities as a pathway to increasing its performance (Ireland, Covin, & Kuratko, 2009). Therefore, the integration of innovation and entrepreneurship for opportunity identification and development and a strategy for sustaining competitive advantage are necessary for value and wealth creation. Organizations that can develop competitive advantages today, while using innovation and entrepreneurship to cultivate tomorrow's advantages, increase the chance of survival and growth in the long term.

Integration of Innovation and Entrepreneurship With Strategy

The integration of innovation and entrepreneurship with strategy can be defined as a vision directed strategic analysis with a core focus on innovative and entrepreneurial behaviors that continuously develop the organization through the identification and development of innovative and entrepreneurial opportunities that result in value creation and sustained competitive advantage. For innovation and entrepreneurship to be ingrained into the very existence of the organization, it must be integrated into the organizational strategy. Organizations like Apple, Dell, and Southwest Airlines capture the essence of a strategy that is unique, innovative, and entrepreneurial in defining and creating market value.

The integration of innovation and entrepreneurship with strategy allows top management to develop strategies that concentrate on (1) competitive advantages that are a core part of strategic management and (2) the identification and development of opportunities for which future competitive advantages can be developed and sustained. It is the simultaneous use of existing advantages and the identification of future opportunities that sustains competitive advantage and the ability to continuously create value and wealth. The integration is beneficial to SMEs and large corporations as it helps SMEs develop their strategies toward competitive advantage and large corporations to become more innovative and entrepreneurial.

The model presented in Figure 4.1 identifies three core dimensions: (1) innovation and entrepreneurial strategic analysis, (2) strategic choice for value creation and competitiveness, and (3) strategic implementation for wealth creation and sustained competitive advantage. The first dimension specifies the key factors influencing the process at different levels, including environmental factors, organizational factors (behavior and climate), and customers and stakeholders. The second dimension focuses on options and choices available from the analysis, specifically focusing on the utilization of resources and the entrepreneurial actions from the first dimension that are used to develop current opportunities while simultaneously exploring new opportunities that will create value. These actions occur primarily at the organizational level. Finally, the implementation of selected opportunities will create advantages for the organization, customers and stakeholders and society through value creation, knowledge, opportunity, competitiveness, and societal developments.

Figure 4.1 The Integration of Innovation and Entrepreneurship with Strategy

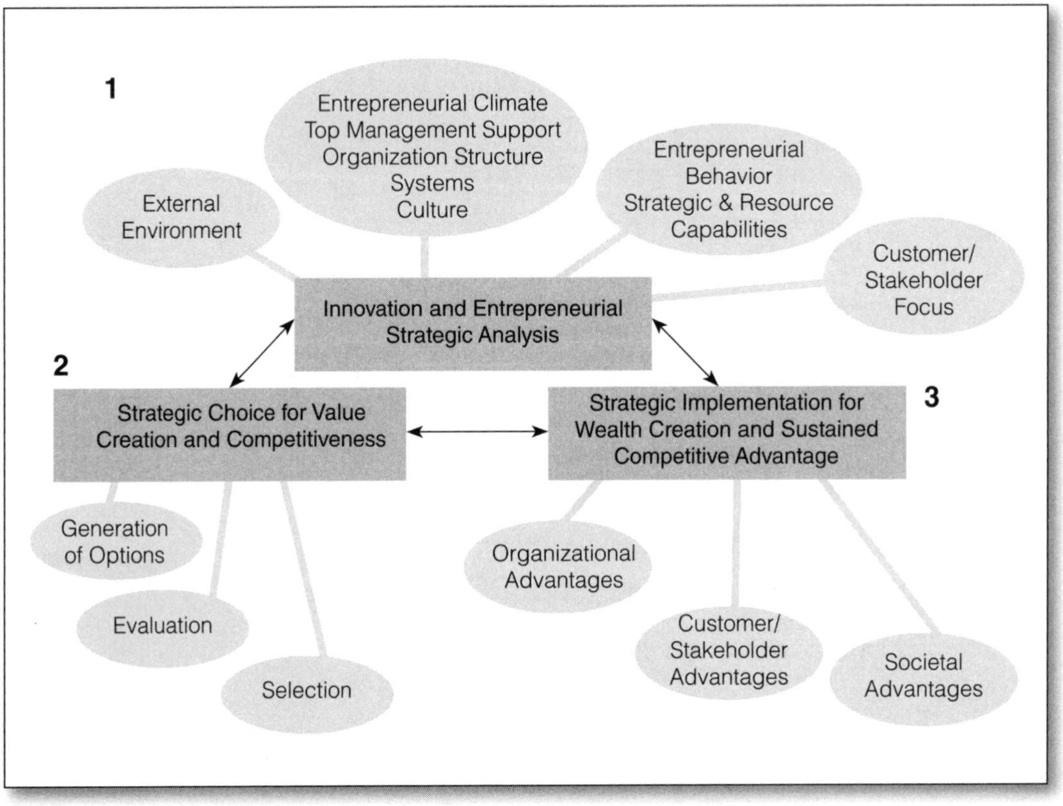

Innovation and Entrepreneurial Strategic Analysis

This analysis involves four main areas: (1) the external environment, (2) the entrepreneurial climate, (3) entrepreneurial behavior, and (4) customer and stakeholder focus.

External Environment

The external environment has been recognized as having a strong influence on the existence and effectiveness of innovation and entrepreneurial activity. Monitoring, assessing, and evaluating the external environment to ensure the right decisions are made and actions implemented is not part of a one-time implementation but needs to be continuous in order to ensure organizational success and competitiveness. Different environmental conditions result in different organizational approaches to innovation and entrepreneurship. In times of economic growth and prosperity, innovation and entrepreneurship emerge as a result of key opportunities. During economic recession, innovation and entrepreneurship occur out of necessity as market conditions significantly change and competition is intensified; only the innovative organization will survive.

The external environment affects an organization's ability to identify or create opportunities and subsequently their ability to develop those opportunities in a competitive advantage. *Munificence, dynamism, hostility,* and *interconnectedness* are important environmental factors for the integration of innovation and entrepreneurship with strategy. Environmental munificence facilitates acquiring resources and the identification of opportunities in addition to the ability to develop the resources and opportunities to create competitive advantage. Organizations seek out environmental munificence, which refers to the level of resources in a particular environment that can support sustained growth, stability, and survival (Dess & Beard, 1984). The environment many organizations face is inherently dynamic and uncertain. Dynamism refers to the extent to which an organization's operating environment is rapidly changing and subject to high levels of uncertainty. This uncertainty results in an inability to adequately access external environmental conditions, creating ambiguity during the strategic decision-making process. This results in decision makers lacking adequate knowledge for identifying and developing new opportunities. Research has shown that organizations frequently respond to challenging environmental conditions such as those present in dynamic environments by innovating and engaging in entrepreneurial behaviors. Hostile environments incentivize organizations to pursue innovation as a source of competitive advantage. Hostility tends to create threats for the organization and stimulates the pursuit of innovation and entrepreneurship. Theories of interconnectedness, including networks and social capital, explain the paths organizations pursue to build capabilities. Open innovation, discussed in Chapter 3, in which large corporations and SMEs share ideas, knowledge, skills, and opportunities, supports the integration of innovation and entrepreneurship with strategy. Ford engages customers in "what's next," taking the organization's open innovation model to the next level; Philips has established partnerships all over the innovation stages from basic innovation to commercialization; **Telefónica** has established a network that involves over 1,000 partners, and they have seven research centers mostly in

Spain and close to technology parks. By applying ideas from its collaborative network, an organization can fill the innovation gap and maintain the balance between their search to achieve competitive advantage as well as identify and develop opportunities and therefore maintain the entrepreneurial mind-set needed for effective integration. SMEs are able to use creativity to create unique innovation while reducing any inhibiting factors associated with their size and limited resources. As a result of slack resources, large corporations are able to explore opportunities outside their traditional domain and in the process can leverage existing business practices.

Entrepreneurial Climate

An entrepreneurial climate reinforces the development of expected behaviors among individuals throughout the organization. To integrate innovation and entrepreneurship with strategy requires an entrepreneurial climate that (1) is supported and facilitated by top management with an entrepreneurial vision; (2) promotes entrepreneurial actions by pursuing and encouraging the pursuit of innovative and entrepreneurial opportunities that can create new business for the organization or increase competitiveness in the existing business domains; and (3) implements the innovative and entrepreneurial actions through the organization's core competencies, which can be used to develop opportunities for competitive advantage. Top management is responsible for developing an entrepreneurial climate that is supported with the appropriate structure, systems and culture.

Entrepreneurial Behavior

Entrepreneurial behavior is seen as an important path to improved performance in all types of organizations. Entrepreneurial behavior and strategic and resource capabilities are important for an organization to develop opportunities and achieve competitive advantage as the sources of its long-term success. The entrepreneurial mind-set is manifested through many specific actions. Entrepreneurial alertness, entrepreneurial self-efficacy, and entrepreneurial effectuation are individual level indicators of entrepreneurial behavior. Their measures are grounded in individual level psychological and cognitive theories. Entrepreneurial alertness entails the ability to notice opportunities that have been overlooked. Entrepreneurial leaders with high self-efficacy frequently contribute to enhanced revenue and employment growth in the organization.

Drive, passion, and entrepreneurial self-efficacy motivate managers to pursue and realize strategic and entrepreneurial goals that are fundamental to the integration of innovation and entrepreneurship with strategy. Effectuation argues that experts use logic to transform means into new outcomes that they themselves may not have initially anticipated. Cognitive ability to effectuate is used to create opportunities in the environment and to achieve short-term competitive advantages. The motivation and encouragement for innovation and entrepreneurship, combined with the utilization of resources and capabilities, foster an innovative and entrepreneurial culture in the organization and the development of market niches in the environment over time that contributes to value and wealth creation.

Customer and Stakeholder Focus

To benefit from the integration of innovation and entrepreneurship with strategy, the focus must be on achieving an array of objectives that are important to customers and stakeholders. An organization must know what customers value and identify the needs of their customers and then create the differentiated products and services to match those needs. When an organization not only satisfies but exceeds the demands of their customers, they are differentiating themselves from average performers and giving themselves greater opportunity for long-term growth and sustained competitive advantage. If SMEs and large corporations do not engage in opportunity identification and development, an innovative, entrepreneurial organization will introduce a better product that provides more value to customers and take their market away. The unique approach to video rental introduced by Netflix drove Blockbuster into bankruptcy. Similarly, iTunes has taken the market of major music stores, creating closures worldwide.

Strategic Choice for Value Creation and Competitiveness

Based on the innovation and entrepreneurial strategic analysis, top management must make strategic choices that will create value and achieve competitive advantages with the objective of being sustained over time. Top management actions must be comprehensive in synchronizing the various resources while simultaneously addressing both strengths and weaknesses to realize competitive advantages that help them pursue future opportunities leading to sustained competitive advantage and value creation.

Strategic Implementation for Value Creation and Sustained Competitive Advantage

The closer the organization's strategy is linked to their core competencies and integrated with the internal activities, the easier it will be to implement. The implementation of a strategy that is integrated with innovation and entrepreneurship requires flexibility and adaptability. A truly innovative and entrepreneurial organization that is focused on creating value and sustained competitive advantage recognizes that implementation involves an iterative process; this organization makes all the necessary adjustments to make their strategy successful. A successful strategy creates advantages for the organization, customers and stakeholders, and society.

Organizational Advantages

New technology and innovation is critical for most all organizations. Many organizations are building relationships with university technology development programs as an external source for new technologies and products. Simultaneously, an increasing number of universities have built technology transfer programs in which they develop new technologies and transfer them to the private sector for commercialization. As such, the university becomes a source of R & D for these organizations. Some organizations use acquisitions to gain access to new technologies and highly valuable innovations. These acquisitions are common in the pharmaceutical industry and in other high-technology industries such as software development. Acquisitions are frequently practiced by technology-oriented organizations such as Microsoft and Cisco, with the objective of gaining access to new software ideas and technologies. Another advantage of developing new technologies and innovation is the creation of new knowledge, which usually leads to new market opportunities and contributes to competitive advantage.

Customer/Stakeholder Advantages

Sound implementation is one that focuses on providing value for customers, building value for stockholders, and generating benefits for other stakeholders and wider community. Successful innovations generate new value for customers and stakeholders. Competitors identify the opportunity created by some innovations and aim to develop a modified version that provides customers with goods or services that have greater reliability, customization, accessibility, higher quality, excellent customer service, and a lower cost than other competing organizations.

Societal Advantages

Innovation and entrepreneurial activities are a major contributor to bringing about economic growth and development, creating new jobs, and enhancing market value. Novel innovations can be used to address a number of environmental issues. Innovation and entrepreneurial activity can help build new economic, social, institutional, and cultural environments and thereby provide significant benefits to society at large.

Top Management Support

Top management support as well as the appropriate organizational structure, systems, and culture are necessary ingredients for the integration of innovation and entrepreneurship with strategy. In an innovative and entrepreneurial organization, top management influences and motivates individuals to identify and develop opportunities in search of competitive advantage.

While structures and systems are necessary for the management and control of an organization, they need to have some flexibility for innovation and entrepreneurship to develop. Strategic flexibility involves a willingness to continuously rethink and make appropriate adjustments to the organization's strategies, structure, systems, and culture. Research has found that an innovative and entrepreneurial organization is more adaptable and flexible to change with decentralized decision making; fewer organizational layers; open channels of communication; and closely integrated R & D, manufacturing, and marketing functions. This flexibility allows an organization to quickly respond to the fast-changing dynamic and complex external environment, thereby creating a position where opportunities can be more readily identified and developed with greater potential to develop competitiveness compared to more bureaucratic organizations.

Culture influences a number of aspects of organizational activity including how people behave and interact. Truly entrepreneurial organizations need to have innovation and entrepreneurship as the core element of their culture. Positive cultures are in line with the organization's vision, mission, and strategies and help promote desired behavior. Top management must manage a culture that applauds successes, learns from failures, and provides screening mechanisms to facilitate innovation and entrepreneurship. Failure is a necessary part of the innovation process because from failure comes the greatest learning and the development of new models. This is recognized by many companies such as Amazon, Facebook, and Google. Innovative organizations build and develop the right culture and systems that encourages innovative behaviors as well as being willing to accept failures and learn from them. Innovative companies never make the same mistake twice; they make different ones, and most importantly, they learn from them all.

For organizations to successfully balance identifying and developing opportunities, searching for competitive advantage is necessary but challenging in today's economic environment. Achieving this balance requires a positive culture that is in line with the organization's vision and strategies, top management support, and an organizational structure that is capable of supporting the dual needs of identification and development. The most effective balance between identifying and developing is influenced by competitive environment in which the organization operates. Top management's abilities to strategically structure the resources to develop capabilities that can be effectively leveraged within the existing competitive environment support the organization's efforts to gain competitive advantage and create value and wealth.

Integrating innovation and entrepreneurship with strategy requires a positive culture and an organization to have a supportive top management team and be able to develop the structures and systems that support such a strategy. If, for example, an organization chooses to pursue open innovation as a strategy, there must be a fit between the culture and the strategy, and they must have top management support and be able to develop the capabilities, structures, and systems to support this open/collaborative approach like Xerox. Frequently researchers at Xerox work directly with customers and deploy ethnographic methods to learn about what the customer really wants. The customer is considered a partner in innovation and they encourage what they call "dreaming with customers" about future aspirations.

Building a Customer-Focused Innovative and Entrepreneurial Strategy

Effective innovations create new value for customers and help the organization overcome the challenges that the business may face. Organizations must be creative to develop innovation, and the core of their innovation must be focused on what customers want. Many organizations handle innovation well; this is what gives companies like Amazon, Apple, Facebook, Google, and Procter & Gamble (P&G) a strong competitive advantage. The innovative and entrepreneurial strategy must deliver increasing satisfaction to customers. Organizations must have an innovative and entrepreneurial strategy that provides customers with goods or services that have greater reliability, customization, accessibility, higher quality, and at a lower cost than the leading competitors. This requires analyzing and assessing products and services that the organization offers to its customers and through R & D determine how their value can be maintained and enhanced in the future to an achieve sustained competitive advantage.

The most effective way to think about innovation is to evaluate the customer and their needs, wants, and expectations now and in the next 5 years. Without customers, there is no business. The customer is whom the organization is expected to deliver added value and as someone who expects to receive added value. The focus must be on meeting and exceeding the customers' needs by the innovation. Apple's iPhone, iPod, and iPad are all spectacular innovations. They respond to the desire of consumers, taking the creative technology and applying it with further creativity into new consumer electronic devices. The iPhone, iPod, and iPad are great examples of the power of customer focus. By being connected with its customers and identifying a gap and customer need, Apple could apply its creativity to add value. The innovation did not just happen. It was customer-focused strategy and R & D that was the result of Apple's innovation.

A truly customer-focused organization drives innovation, because innovation is the means by which it satisfies the unmet demands of its customers. Creating structures and systems to empower people to be innovative and entrepreneurial is one of the most effective ways for organizations to activate the creative energies of their people. Combined with top management support and commitment, empowerment gives people the freedom and flexibility to take responsibility for innovation and entrepreneurship. Empowerment in the presence of a strong innovative culture produces energy and enthusiasm to consistently work toward producing innovative outcomes that are aligned with external factors and customer demands.

Summary

The increasingly dynamic, complex, and competitive external environment generates significant challenges for organizations today. Organizations that are adaptable, flexible, responsive to opportunities, innovative, and entrepreneurial are in a stronger position not only to adjust to this environment but to embrace it and seek and develop the opportunities that achieve their goal to create value and sustainable competitive advantage. No organization is isolated from its external environment, and each must be able to adapt with appropriate strategies.

The integration of innovation and entrepreneurship with strategy gives the organization greater potential to identify and develop opportunities that enhance their competitiveness and create more value. The core objective of strategic management is to successfully develop a strong competitive advantage. Innovation and entrepreneurship are concerned with identifying opportunities that can be effectively developed through the organization's competitive advantages resulting in enhanced value. Competitors are anyone your customer has access to that can fulfill the same need.

Sustaining innovative and entrepreneurial behavior is the result of top management support and encouragement throughout the organization regarding the value of entrepreneurial actions in creating value and gaining competitive advantage. Supportive organizational structure and systems that are flexible and adaptive are fundamental for innovative and entrepreneurial organizations to achieve the balance between opportunity identification and development. Innovation and entrepreneurship must be embedded into the culture of the organization. Top management needs to recognize the importance of developing and supporting a culture through which innovative and entrepreneurial activities are necessary to create value. The culture must (1) eliminate obstacles that inhibit opportunities, (2) promote teamwork, (3) ensure availability of resources, (4) learn from failure, (5) be flexible, and (6) be totally committed to opportunity identification and development.

The organization should have identified the needs of the customers and have created innovative products and services to match those needs. When an organization satisfies and is capable of exceeding customer needs, they are differentiating themselves from average performers and giving themselves greater opportunity for long-term growth and survival. By doing this, they are putting themselves in a stronger position to attract customers, stakeholders, and suppliers. It is the role and responsibility of strategic management to integrate innovation and entrepreneurship with a strategy that motivates and inspires individuals and teams at all levels to be creative and innovative.

References

Dess, G., & Beard, D. (1984). Dimensions of organizational task environments. *Administrative Science Quarterly, 29*(1), 52–73.

Ireland, D. R., Covin, J. G., & Kuratko, D. F. (2009). Conceptualizing corporate entrepreneurship strategy. *Entrepreneurship Theory and Practice, 33*(1), 19–46.

Kuratko, D. F., & Audretsch, D.B. (2009). Strategic entrepreneurship: Exploring different perspectives of an emerging concept. *Entrepreneurship Theory and Practice, 33*(1), 1–17.

Porter, M. E. (1980). *Competitive strategy.* New York: Free Press.

Porter, M. E. (1996). What is strategy? *Harvard Business Review, 74,* 61–78.

Suggested Readings

Hitt M. A., Ireland, D. R., Sirmon, D. G., & Trahms, C. A. (2011). Strategic entrepreneurship: Creating value for individuals, organizations and society. *Academy of Management Perspectives, 25*(2), 57–75.

The authors examine the contributions of strategic management and entrepreneurship to strategic entrepreneurship. The authors extend the understanding of the strategic entrepreneurship construct by building on a previous model of strategic entrepreneurship—to develop an input-process-output model. They examine the resource inputs into strategic entrepreneurship and explore the resource orchestration processes that are important for strategic entrepreneurship and the outcomes. Overall in their model of strategic entrepreneurship they incorporate multilevel outcomes that motivate entrepreneurs.

Hornsby, J. S., Kuratko, D. F., Shepherd, D. A., & Bott, J. P. (2009). Managers' corporate entrepreneurial actions: Examining perception and position. *Journal of Business Venturing, 24*(3), 236–247.

In this article, the authors use corporate entrepreneurship (CE) and managerial levels literature to propose that managers differ in structural ability to make the most of their organizational environment. Their analysis found that the relationship between managers' perceptions of the organizational environment and the number of entrepreneurial ideas implemented varied across managers of different structural levels. Overall, their findings suggest that managerial levels provide a structural ability to "make more of" organizational factors that facilitate entrepreneurial action.

Ireland, R. D., Covin, J. G., & Kuratko, D. F. (2009). Conceptualizing corporate entrepreneurship strategy. *Entrepreneurship Theory and Practice, 31*(1), 19–46.

In this article, the authors conceptualize the components of CE strategy as fundamental for integrating key elements within CE's domain. Their CE strategy model has three main components that include (1) the antecedents of CE strategy, (2) the elements of CE, and (3) the outcomes of CE strategy. They discuss the contribution of this model to the CE literature and how it differentiates from previous models.

Kelley, J. D. & Lee, H. (2010). Managing innovation champions: The impact of project characteristics on the direct manager role. *Journal of Product Innovation Management, 27*(7), 1007–1019.

The authors investigate when to lend direct managerial support—and how much support—to those championing such projects. Their research provides insights into the connection between project characteristics and the level of direct manager involvement. Overall, the article suggests that both empowerment and the role of a manager are important to the management of innovation.

Somaya, D., Teece, D., & Wakeman. S. (2012). Innovation in multi-invention contexts: Mapping solutions to technological and intellectual property complexity. *California Management Review, 53*(4), 47–79.

This article suggests that business firms need to develop a patent strategy that is aligned with their overall organizational objectives and that helps proactively direct their innovative activity. The authors develop a framework to help innovative firms and technology users frame the relevant issues and achieve viable strategies, appropriate structures, and workable solutions.

Terziovski, M. (2010). Research notes and commentaries innovation practice and its performance implications in small and medium enterprises (SMEs) in the manufacturing sector: A resource-based view. *Strategic Management Journal, 31*(8), 892–902.

The author in this article identifies innovation drivers and their performance implications in manufacturing SMEs. The research found that SMEs are similar to large firms with respect to the way that innovation strategy and formal structure are the key drivers of their performance but do not appear to utilize innovation culture in a strategic and structured manner. Overall, the author concludes that SMEs' performance is likely to improve as there is an increase in the degree to which they mirror large manufacturing firms with respect to formal strategy and structure and to which they recognize that innovation culture and strategy are closely aligned throughout the innovation process.

CHAPTER 5

Developing Innovation and Entrepreneurship in Both Individuals and Teams

H ow can organizations develop innovations through individuals and teams that meet customer demands? What entrepreneurial behaviors are important for individuals and teams to identify and exploit opportunities? How can an organization integrate entrepreneurship and marketing so that they are more market oriented and customer focused in their innovations? Should customer focus be a key driving force for innovation and entrepreneurship within an organization?

Scenario: L'Oréal

L'Oréal is one of the largest companies in France and the world's biggest manufacturer of high quality cosmetics and perfumes, producing brands such as Ambre Solaire, Cacharel, Garnier, Giorgio Armani, Lancôme, Redken, Vichy, and YSL. It has a global distribution network and the industry's highest research and development (R & D) budget. L'Oréal was founded in 1909 by Eugène Schueller. In 1907, Schueller demonstrated his drive and ability for new ideas by developing his first hair dye formula under the name Oréal. The dyes were an exceptional breakthrough of their time. Since its foundation, L'Oréal has undertaken its adventure in the beauty industry to be the world's leading cosmetic company. The core focus of L'Oréal is innovation; excellence by increasingly safe, imaginative, and effective products; the ability to meet the diverse needs of people worldwide; and their purpose being met by combining economic growth, ethics, social, and environmental responsibility.

From 1909 to 1956, L'Oréal hair dyes were a huge success and were expanding beyond France to Italy in 1910; Austria in 1911; the Netherlands in 1913; and then the United States, Canada, the United Kingdom, and Brazil. Schueller's industry success enhanced his belief that research and innovation is the core for growth and success. This belief accelerated his continuous innovation in the beauty industry. In 1931, Schueller focused on developing promotional events and inventing new advertising strategies. He was the first to air a commercial that was sung rather than spoken in 1932. Schueller believed in two types of advertising: one was designed to raise interest and the other was designed to maximize sales. On April 4, 1939, the Société des Teintures Inoffensives pour Cheveux officially changed its name to L'Oréal, with offices at 14 Rue Royale in Paris, which remains the company's head office today. In 1940, L'Oréal was marketing highly sophisticated products and the number of women's hair salons was growing. L'Oréal became the preferred brand for hairstylists. A key stage for L'Oréal's international growth came in 1954. After 3 years of market research in the United States, COSMAIR became the representative for L'Oréal hair products in the United States. This marked a significant international milestone in company growth.

Between 1957 and 1983, there was significant growth through the acquisitions of strategic brands. Following the death of Eugène Schueller in 1957, François Dalle was appointed chairman and managing director. Dalle was a visionary and was targeting a number of acquisitions in order to expand the group's positions in new market sectors and new distribution channels, developing research, driving internal growth, increasing the group's international presence, and making beauty more accessible to win new consumers. In response to the 1950s boom, L'Oréal, present in the Brazilian market since the late 1930s, established a direct presence in the country in 1959 forming FAPROCO (Fábrica Produtos Cosméticos S.A.). Today, L'Oréal Brazil is an export platform for all of Latin America. In 1961, L'Oréal bought Cadoricin and acquired a controlling stake in LaSCAD to gain a foothold in the significant market for "mass-market" cosmetics sold in a large number of outlets. This was L'Oréal's initial entry into mass-market retail. In 1963, L'Oréal Group was listed on the Paris Stock Exchange, which gave them access to new financial resources. The acquisitions of Lancôme in 1964 was their first step to becoming a luxury goods empire, and Garnier, in 1965, enabled L'Oréal to gain a portfolio of complementary hair care products with an organic positioning, which created a distinct approach to hair care.

With more resources and expertise, L'Oréal launched numerous successful products, many of which continue to be market leaders. The acquisition of Biotherm in 1970 stepped up L'Oréal's research effort. In 1973, L'Oréal acquired a majority interest in the pharmaceutical company Synthélabo, giving L'Oréal the opportunity to develop their dermatological and dermopharmaceutical activities. With the acquisition of Gemey in 1973, L'Oréal gained a significant position in the volume retailing makeup market in its native country. In 1974, they signed an agreement with Nestlé, which was beneficial to L'Oréal's international development—particularly Japan, the future of L'Oréal's expansion in Asia. L'Oréal's earnings grew twice as fast as the average in the cosmetics industry. Their success allowed greater commitment to R & D, and in 1979 in conjunction with Nestlé, they established the International Dermatological Research Centre (CIRD) near Nice (France). François Dalle set up an applied R & D center for hair and skin care to tailor L'Oréal's products to the Japanese market in 1983.

Between 1984 and 2000, there was further growth for L'Oréal, which was predominately driven by their significant investment in research. In addition, the strategic product launches also strengthened their brand image. In 1985, L'Oréal obtained the Ralph Lauren license, an acquisition that anchored L'Oréal's position in the luxury products market in the United States and in luxury men's fragrances. Also in 1985, Biotherm created the first line of skin care products designed exclusively for men. Charles Zviak was chief executive officer from 1984 to 1988. His focus was on the research/marketing relationship, which promotes ongoing exchange between research and current marketing trends. Lindsay Owen-Jones became chief executive officer in 1988 and brought about significant transformation. L'Oréal's scope changed to become the world leader in cosmetics through the global presence of its brands and strategic acquisitions. He developed the market by providing a balanced range of activities, centered on hair care, hair color, skin care, makeup, and perfume.

Two acquisitions took place in 1989: one with Helena Rubinstein, the American brand of skin care products, and the other with La Roche-Posay, a high-tech dermatological product that is recommended worldwide by dermatologists. The acquisition of Redken occurred in 1993. L'Oréal undertook a series of strategic acquisitions in the United States to enable them to develop their Professional Products Division and after Paris make the United States the second stronghold in the world for L'Oréal. In 1994, L'Oréal was the first international cosmetic company that the Indian government granted the status of wholly owned subsidiary. This provided great opportunity in a country experiencing substantial economic growth.

The acquisition of Maybelline in 1996, the leader in mass-market makeup in the United States, was an important strategic move. Another acquisition took place in 1998 with SoftSheen in the United States—the brand for ethnic hair types—giving them singular expertise in ethnic hair care. L'Oréal acquired four companies in 2000; the first was Carson, which provided them with an opportunity to strengthen their presence on the continent. The second was Kiehl's, a niche brand in the luxury market. The third was Matrix, the number one professional hair care product in the United States. The fourth was Dermablend, an American brand created by a dermatologist to cover facial blemishes, such as angioma or scars. In 2000, L'Oréal's first Code of Business Ethics was launched, which formalized its values and principles.

L'Oréal entered the 21st century by eagerly accepting diversity in its global growth agenda. It developed further acquisitions in their goal to cover the world's diverse cosmetic requirements and to undertake new socially responsible initiatives in the interests of sustainable development. L'Oréal joined the World Business Council for Sustainable Development in 2001 with the objective of fostering best practices in environmental, economic, and social issues. The acquisition with Biomedic, an American brand of professional products for aesthetic correction, took place in 2001. L'Oréal, along with 2,000 other companies, expressed social responsibility and joined the UN Global Compact in 2002. In 2003, to speed up Garnier's rollout in China, L'Oréal engaged in an acquisition with Mininurse in China. The Research Institute for Ethnic Skin and Hair opened in Chicago in 2003. In 2006, Jean-Paul Agon was appointed chief executive officer with responsibility for the group's operational management. An acquisition with The Body Shop in 2006 provided L'Oréal with new inspiration and experience for its sustainable development initiatives. In 2008, an acquisition of YSL Beauté—and its crown jewel YSL—joined L'Oréal's Luxury Products Division. With this strategic acquisition, L'Oréal opened a new chapter in its history with the aspiration to become a world leader in selective distribution.

L'Oréal employs 66,600 people worldwide and distributes their products in 130 countries. They have 23 global brands with annual sales for these brands of over €50 million. In 2010, they had €19.5 billion consolidated sales, filed 612 patents, and have 100 active cooperation agreements with leading academic and research institutions. L'Oréal is committed to research and innovation, which has 3,420 employees of 60 different nationalities working in 30 different disciplines. In 2010, they invested €665 million in cosmetic and dermatological research. They have 18 research centers worldwide and 12 evaluation centers. They are customer-focused and constantly aware of what women and men worldwide want and aim to anticipate their expectations. One third of the research and innovation budget is devoted to advanced research. L'Oréal makes a powerful statement of social responsibility and takes a major step forward as a corporate citizen. They are ranked among the 100 most sustainable and ethical companies in the world.

Innovative and entrepreneurial organizations like L'Oréal are internationally goal directed and customer focused. They leverage their people and R & D to be innovative and entrepreneurial through flexibility, responsiveness, and openness to the ever-changing demands, expectations, and international diversity of customers all over the world.

Introduction

The challenge facing many organizations in today's dynamic and competitive environment is how to continuously develop creativity and innovation through people that meet and exceed customers' expectations. Organizations operate in very diverse domains and meet the demands of multiple customers and stakeholders. The ability of an organization to meet these demands depends to a large extent on their ability to utilize all resources efficiently and effectively. Innovation and entrepreneurship is not possible without people. The types of people involved in the innovation process and how they are organized has a significant impact on the organization's innovation performance and its ability to be competitive. With more intensified competition, the inevitable result will be increasing difficulties in winning market share and difficulties in obtaining a larger share of the market. These difficulties are intensified if organizations are not utilizing the competencies and creativity of their people to identify opportunities that will be embraced by customers.

While organizations have no control over the external environment, they can select and support entrepreneurial individuals and team level creativity and encourage teamwork in a multidisciplined approach that is market oriented and customer focused. An entrepreneurial organization achieves competitive advantage with continuous development of product, service, and process innovations. However, this must meet and exceed the needs of the market and customers in order to be competitive. L'Oréal is an excellent example of a global organization that has an in-depth, well-researched understanding of what customers want. The company is succeeding through instilling innovation and reaping the benefits through market share and competitiveness. Their market strategy uses innovation to create differentiated products that drive growth. Specifically, as environments become more dynamic, threatening, and complex, there is a greater need for innovation and entrepreneurship as traditional managerial orientations are not sufficient. The result is all too frequently a loss in market position, declining profits, or more significantly business failure. Entrepreneurship and marketing are approached as proactive organizational responses to an increasingly dynamic and complex external environment.

For organizations to develop and grow in today's environments, as well as adopt the appropriate strategies, structures, systems, and cultures that support and facilitate innovation and entrepreneurial activities (as discussed in Chapter 4), they need people who are driven, motivated, adaptable to change, market oriented, and customer focused. They also need to demonstrate entrepreneurial behaviors and values.

This chapter examines the importance for an organization to develop innovation and entrepreneurship among their people to ensure that they are responsive to the needs of the market to survive and grow. Effectiveness in innovation and entrepreneurship is discussed to provide an understanding of the importance of people within the organization who have the competencies and are supported by the organization to champion opportunities and totally satisfy customer expectations. Entrepreneurship and marketing as two fundamental organizational disciplines are first discussed. Then there is a discussion on the importance of alignment between the entrepreneurial orientation (EO) and market orientation (MO) so that innovations are market oriented and customer focused, thus enhancing value and competitiveness. The link among EO, MO, and learning is presented—as learning supports the organization's innovation and entrepreneurship by concentrating on market and customer activities. Following a discussion on the market and customer analysis for innovative and entrepreneurial activities, this chapter concludes by discussing innovation and entrepreneurship in challenging economic times.

Innovation and Entrepreneurship Among Individuals and Teams

Talented people are the most important source of competitive advantage for every organization—particularly those in high-technology industries that compete on creativity and innovation. Having the right people and skills necessitate investing in individuals, providing proper training and development, and creating a continuous learning organization. The challenge organizations face is how to enable people within the organization to deploy their creativity and share their competencies to bring about innovations that enhance competitiveness. Innovative organizations are ones that have a supportive top management team that is more adaptable to change, with decentralized decision making, flexible organizational structures, open channels of communication, a culture that is conducive to innovative and entrepreneurial activity and have closely integrated R & D, manufacturing, and marketing functions (as discussed in Chapter 4). These systems will not work without people who will recognize and champion opportunities in light of market conditions and customer needs. Companies must provide the resources to facilitate the efforts of their talented people.

Developing innovation and entrepreneurship through people requires the following:

- Individuals who have the knowledge, skills, ability, energy, drive, and passion to seek and exploit opportunities
- Teams within departments, cross-functional and interorganizational level working together to achieve synergy. This requires investing in team building and utilizing the competencies of individuals with different specializations at different levels
- Individual and team development through commitment to training and development to ensure high levels of competence and skills
- Positive approach to creative ideas—supported by motivation and reward systems
- Learning organization that encourages and supports high levels of interaction within the internal and external organization to share experiences and knowledge and keep ahead of the competition in anticipating customers' needs

Individuals and teams must be well apprised of their organization's capabilities to satisfy customers' requirements. They are one of the organization's most significant information processors. What distinguishes innovative and entrepreneurial individuals and teams from those that are not is their use and ability to identify opportunities with the help of boundary spanning (the practice of relating to people outside the organization to yield better overall decision making), translate environmental information for the organization, and use rich information in the organization's decision making. However, the application of innovative and entrepreneurial thinking to the organization's core strategy is primarily dealing with external questions. Where is there a gap in the market? Does this mean there is actually a market large enough in this identified gap? How can the organization continuously differentiate itself? What does the customer really want?

Developing individuals and teams to be more innovative and entrepreneurial will improve an organization's ability to redirect and focus resources effectively and faster than competitors because it allows all members of the organization to respond to the needs for change and make appropriate changes ahead of competitors. As indicated in Figure 5.1, this in turn can enhance performance and competitiveness; increase responsiveness to both the market and the customer; and increase the number of successful innovations as well as improve the drive, motivation, and satisfaction among workers. An organization that develops and supports individuals and teams to be more innovative and entrepreneurial are enhancing their chances of gaining and sustaining competitive advantage in challenging market conditions.

Successful organizations recognize that they cannot outperform their competitors in all aspects of business. They instead focus on their most

Figure 5.1 Individual and Team Effectiveness in Innovation and Entrepreneurship

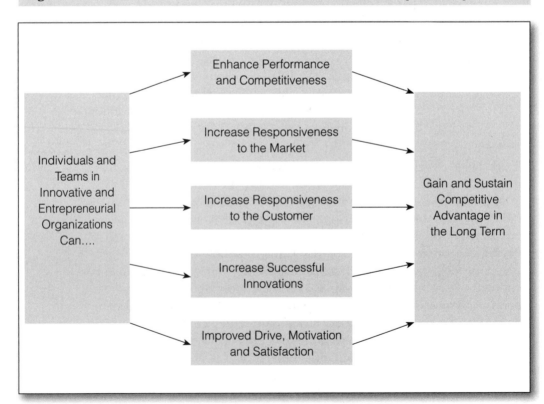

important innovations and their development. L'Oréal's international expansion has allowed them to gain in-depth knowledge of their target markets. They consistently improve their understanding of consumer preferences and ensure that their market position highlights that understanding. In a dynamic, complex, and increasingly competitive environment where the supply of products and services in many cases far exceed the demand, customer satisfaction and customer retention are no longer matters of choice but of survival.

Entrepreneurship and Marketing

Entrepreneurship and marketing are two fundamental organizational disciplines that bring distinctive yet compatible approaches to deal with customers' needs and the objective of creating customer value. The entrepreneurship process includes activities that people within an organization seek to satisfy customer needs through innovations that achieve greater efficiency and effectiveness. Innovative and entrepreneurial organizations identify opportunities, innovate, facilitate, and support the development of these opportunities. They consider changes in the external environment as an opportunity to address market needs and frequently assume that such external environmental changes will create new markets of customers without comprehensively analyzing the relationship between the opportunity and the market. For example, does the opportunity mean that there is an actual market? What are the specific market needs? What is the customer distribution in the market? While there may be a gap in the market resulting in an opportunity, this does not necessarily guarantee that there is a market in the gap for which the opportunity can be successfully developed.

Marketing focuses on identifying and understanding the market aspect of opportunities and the customer and then translating customer needs into new products or services. While opportunities may emerge as a result of changes in the external environmental conditions, the potential to create value, as a core aspect of the opportunity, ultimately depends on the existence of a market and the ability of the organization to provide a product or service that satisfies customers. Organizations that develop an understanding of customers' existing and future needs enhance their ability to exploit opportunities and serve markets. Marketing provides various ways through which organizations can understand customer needs such as broad market research, market and customer analysis, customer interactions, and users as innovators. At L'Oréal, new ideas are emanating in emerging markets. New products are developed to meet local needs and then developed in more mature markets. L'Oréal recognizes and exploits opportunities such as new market segments (Asia-Pacific, Latin America, the Middle East, and Africa), which then became their leading growth drivers of 2012.

Entrepreneurship and marketing opportunity provide a valuable knowledge of how organizations deal with market needs. Organizations with effective promotion of brand-name products, customer services, and innovative merchandising such as Apple, Procter & Gamble (P&G), Polo Ralph Lauren, and Zara perform well compared to competitors by adding unique value to products and services through innovations that are market oriented. Since customer needs are constantly changing in order to sustain competitiveness, the core link that needs to be established between entrepreneurship and marketing is value creation. Value is created by tapping into unique opportunities and being highly sophisticated in the use of modern marketing techniques. This enhances the organization's competitiveness by identifying and exploiting opportunities that meet and exceed customer requirements.

Organizational Alignment of Entrepreneurial Orientation and Market Orientation

EO reflects the objectives of the organization in relation to the process of identifying and exploiting market opportunities. EO is appropriate to assess an organization's overall level of entrepreneurial processes and behaviors. EO is a central component of entrepreneurship and strategy research that was conceptualized to have three key dimensions: (1) innovation, (2) risk-taking, and (3) proactiveness (Covin & Slevin, 1989; Miller, 1983). Innovation refers to an organization's commitment to (1) seeking and supporting new, unusual, or novel ideas; (2) being creative; and (3) experimenting in the development of new products, services, and processes. The risk-taking dimension is the extent that organizations are willing to commit significant resources to uncertain projects where outcomes are unknown and the risk of failure is costly. Proactiveness is the extent to which an organization supports and facilitates the development and implementation of innovations through whatever means are necessary.

Certain environmental conditions facilitate high levels of EO than other environments. Previous research has found that organizations with a high level of EO have the ability to make uncertain and turbulent environments work to their benefit. Environmental dynamism, hostility, complexity, and heterogeneity have been associated with higher levels of EO in successful organizations. Virgin Airlines' focus on autonomy and proactiveness and Sony's commitment to innovation and risk-taking are indicative of a strong EO. Sony is internationally recognized for producing innovative, high quality products, such as the VAIO laptop, PlayStation video game console, and Cyber-shot camera models. Sony aims to increase customer satisfaction through innovative products that are specialized, differentiated, and miniature. Some of the most innovative and entrepreneurial organizations are renowned leaders in their field, creating products that the majority of consumers have used. These include Apple, Intel, Microsoft, Panasonic, and Sony. 3M has a great reputation for effective innovation that is globally recognized; the company's policies create a climate for creativity and innovation.

MO reflects the organization's philosophy to identify and meet the needs and requirements of customers by being adaptive in responding to market conditions. MO focuses on continuously gathering information regarding target customer needs and the competitor's position and capabilities and then using these insights to make decisions that will create superior customer value. MO gives rise to innovative behaviors that focus on understanding the needs of customers; this is particularly important in uncertain and turbulent environments that are subject to rapid change. It is usually measured by evaluating the organization's commitment to focus strategic decisions based on the customer, and the market as customer satisfaction is a key organizational objective as evident in the case of L'Oréal. It is customer, competitor, and opportunity focused. Marketing activities strongly influence the entrepreneurial process. MO encourages and supports the exploitation of innovative opportunities to meet current market needs.

The entrepreneurial process starts with opportunity alertness. This refers to an individual's inherent motivation and ability to recognize opportunities. The opportunity-seeking behavior can involve being alert to existing opportunities or creating new opportunities. Innovative and entrepreneurial organizations are constantly seeking opportunities, observing everyday experiences, experimenting with new experiences, and networking with diverse groups of individuals inside and outside the organization. Previous research suggests that an organization's MO enhances its ability to recognize opportunities. MO captures an organization's understanding of the market and competitors, and facilitates the organization's ability to effectively differentiate itself. Organizations with stronger MO enhance opportunity alertness through intelligence dissemination and organizational responsiveness, generating interactions that enable opportunities to be addressed and evaluated.

Successful opportunity recognition needs organizational behaviors characterized by search, discovery, experimentation, risk-taking, and innovation. Opportunity recognition involves determining if core market needs exist and if value can be created by satisfying these needs through existing internal competencies. Having market knowledge on existing unmet needs provides the organization with appropriate knowledge and insight to identify novel and meaningful ways to satisfy customers' needs, enhancing the organization's creativity resulting in more effective innovations.

Opportunity realization suggests organizational behaviors characterized by refinement, implementation, efficiency, effectiveness, and production. It incorporates the organization of activities around the innovation—for example, gathering and utilizing resources to organize around the innovation. These activities bring the innovation to the market and support its market deployment in order to satisfy customer needs and expectations.

The organizational alignment of EO and MO is a significant factor in its survival, growth, development, and competitiveness. The combination of these orientations provides a more comprehensive understanding of current and future customers, competitors, and environmental conditions.

Entrepreneurial Orientation, Market Orientation, and Learning Link

A link between EO and MO is learning: Learning about markets and customers contributes to the development of EO and MO. The first focus of organizational learning emphasizes information generation and dissemination systems through which learning takes place; this is referred to in the literature as knowledge acquisition. The second focus is the need for a shared mental model, a shared organizational vision, and an open-minded approach to problem solving, which is referred to in the literature as value acquisition. An organization's approach to "the way things are done around here" highlights its values and norms and influences its approach to learning. There is no "one best way" for organizations to learn, and the paths and processes involved in learning can be quite different between organizations. The efficiency and effectiveness of learning is a function of the organization's core values, which is illustrated through the organization's commitment and dedication to learning, open and objective approach, and a shared sense of purpose and direction among individuals at all levels within the organization. Effective organizational learning provides individuals and teams with important information about the gaps and limitations in the organization's market as well as developing their knowledge and competencies. Learning can influence opportunity recognition and innovation—thereby providing additional support in satisfying customer needs. Knowledge gained through learning may include identifying the following:

- An organization's lack of understanding of the core aspects of customer needs
- Any change in customer needs
- Any change in actual customers resulting in new customers with very different needs
- A weak intelligence generation processes

Organizational learning is considered by many as the key to organizational success and the ability to gain knowledge through learning more efficiently and effectively than competitors can be a source of sustainable competitive advantage. Organizational learning is not a one-time implementation or short-term process; rather, it is a continuous process throughout the life of the organization. As an organization grows and develops, learning plays a critical role in enhancing the resources and capabilities of the organization in line with the internal and external demand. The knowledge gained through learning can be utilized to create new innovations and entrepreneurial activity that, in turn, produce new market-oriented contributions that support intelligence generation, dissemination, and organizational responsiveness to emerging opportunities. The more entrepreneurial an organization is, the greater the emphasis on learning and the more likely it is to have a culture that is committed to learning open-minded and shared vision.

Market and Customer Analysis for Innovation and Entrepreneurial Activities

MO and customer focus should be the foundation for an organization's innovation efforts. An organization attains and sustains competitive advantage in its target markets only by exceptional execution in understanding the market and meeting the customers' needs. In relation to responsive MO, there are numerous organizations that are very innovative in their efforts to meet customers' needs. One example is Walmart, which aims to create superior value for customers by primarily focusing on low prices while continuously innovating to be increasingly more efficient and effective in its physical handling and distribution processes. Proactive MO that is focused on the latent needs, provides a deeper understanding of customer needs and, thus, to the development of innovative products and services.

There are highly successful organizations that approach markets differently. For example, organizations like 3M, General Electric (GE), IBM, Nokia, and P&G are very driven by the markets and customers; they are market oriented with entrepreneurial values and more incremental innovations. Alternatively, organizations like Amazon, Dell, IKEA, Ryanair, Southwest Airlines, and Starbucks are more market drivers, aiming to create new customers and markets; these organizations are more entrepreneurial-focused with radical innovations. Both have a very different approach yet are highly successful. From an organizational perspective, it is finding the best approach by taking into account the core strategy of the organization and the external and internal environment.

In analyzing the market and its customer, it is important for an organization to think about the following (see Figure 5.2):

- How big is the market for the new innovation?
- Who are the potential customers, and what evidence is there that they will actually buy the product?
- Why would customers buy the product? What is unique about it compared to competitors, and what are the key success factors (KSFs)?
- Who are the competitors, and what is their competitive position in the market?
- What is the best route to the market?

As indicated in Figure 5.2, market and customer analysis is an assessment of the overall appeal of the market and customers for the proposed innovation. This requires the following:

- Analyzing the key factors influencing the market in the short, medium, and long term
- Understanding the national and international market changes and in particular identifying:
  o What is happening in the leading and most innovative markets?
  o What do customers require in these markets?
  o How are products/services adapting to meet and exceed their needs?
  o Are new competitors entering this market?
  o Are there regulations and standards governing the market and the products?
  o Is the market rapidly changing and, if so, how?

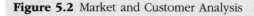
Figure 5.2 Market and Customer Analysis

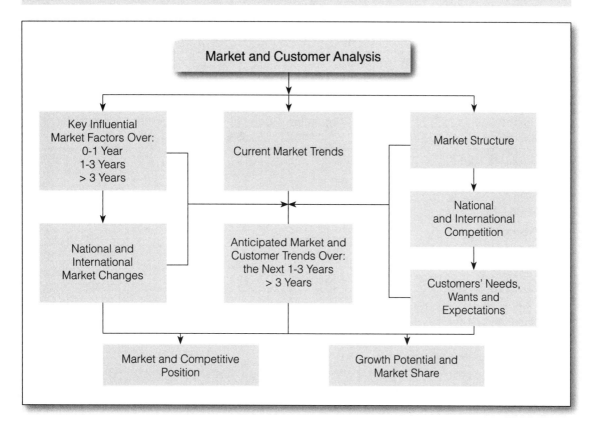

- Assessing the current and anticipated market trends in terms of economics, demographics, lifestyle, deregulation, technological advancement and development, environmental responsibility, and sustainability
- Knowing how the market is structured and if it is feasible to secure a good market position
- Knowing the key competitors both nationally and internationally
- Knowing the customers' real needs, wants, and expectations in terms of products, services, packaging, price, accessibility, and distribution
- Knowing the current market and competitive position in comparison to competitors and how the innovation can enhance this further (see Figure 5.3)
- Knowing the growth potential and market share in the short, medium, and long term

Figure 5.3 Evaluating Your Organizational Innovations against Competitors in the Market

Evaluating Your Organizational Innovation Against the Key Competitors in the Market	Your Company	Competitor 1	Competitor 2	Competitor 3	Competitor 4
Market Position Sales Value/Volume Market Shares Product Range Product Quality Product Price Customer Service and Quality Name and Reputation					
Operations Manufacturing Plant and Equipment Technology Advancement and Development Design and Innovation Cost Efficiency and Effectiveness					
Human Resources Number of Staff Staff Competencies Specialized Training and Development					

Financial Position Sales/Projected Sales Profitability Available Finance Required Finance					
Competitive Position Ability to Sustain Competitiveness					
Core Strengths					
Core Weaknesses					

Interpreting the insights gained for market and customer analysis provides insights into seeking new ways of evaluating the business based on the analysis as follows:

- Knowing the implications of trends and expected changes in the short, medium, and long term
  - Developing scenarios and examining the implications
- Identifying the key issues to be addressed through doing the following:
  - Ensuring activity participation from individuals and teams inside the organization
  - Engaging in open innovation opportunities
  - Identifying lead users who are users and whose current needs will become general in a marketplace in the coming months or years. Since lead users are familiar with conditions that will be evident in the future, they can be an effective *need forecasting laboratory* for marketing research (Von Hippel, 1986)
- Understanding the sources of customer satisfaction and dissatisfaction
- Identifying existing industry traditions that are successful and those that are no longer viable
- Identifying organizational traditions that are no longer working
  - Are there constraints in views that are inhibiting?

- Identifying the key obstacles that are affecting the opportunities of increasing quality, service, sales, profits, growth, and competitiveness
- Identifying any shortcomings vis-à-vis the KSFs
- Reversing roles and stepping into the shoes of (1) competitors and (2) customers to provide new insights and perspectives

Insights gained for analyzing markets and customers provide organizations with opportunities to seek connections and bridge gaps by looking at the following:

- Gaps that can be filled in existing product ranges
- Possible combinations—novel combinations of products, processes, packaging, and so forth—for example, Bailey's Irish Cream is a combination of whiskey and cream and iPhones, smartphones, and even standard mobile phones that are not only phones but also include cameras, music, Internet, and many apps if selected
- Modifications that can be made to existing products or processes
  - o Bigger, smaller, cheaper, alternative uses—for example, desktops, laptops, notebooks, iPads, pocket television
- Knowing what competitors are doing and that things can be modified or adapted
- Analyzing beyond the industry for ideas that could be transferred from other industries
- Evaluating reverse possibilities—for example, prepaid cards verses credit cards, diet chocolate

When an organization is market oriented and customer focused, the knowledge they gain about their customers and competitors results in more effective market targeting, product development, and positioning, thereby creating opportunities for increased competitiveness and sustained competitive advantage. Such organizations as IKEA, Southwest Airlines, and Starbucks are market leaders with sustained competitive advantage. Organizations that have outstanding knowledge about the market and customers are in a stronger position to achieve sustained competitive advantage.

Innovation and Entrepreneurship in Challenging Economic Times

During challenging economic times, organizations need to be even more customer focused. This reemphasizes the importance for organizations to align EO and MO and to recognize viable opportunities that are market oriented and customer focused. For decades, cost and price have been significant in introducing new products, developing new technology, and seeking alternative solutions to existing problems. During the economic boom times from the mid-1990s to mid-2007, the cost–price value component of new product development was less significant, because businesses and customers had greater purchasing power and disposable income. Since the later part of 2007, organizations and customers are more cautious about their ability to spend due to the global economic conditions, unemployment, credit constraints, and uncertainty about the future. The more cautious approach to spending provides major opportunities in such areas as business coaching, discount retailing, luxury products, credit and debt management, virtual meetings, outsourcing, and do-it-yourself culture.

While there are opportunities for innovation and entrepreneurial activity during an economic crisis, they must be market oriented and customer focused. These innovations must be a solution to a pressing problem and must be created for customers who require such products. Extending beyond R & D to open innovation (as discussed in Chapter 3) and into the marketplace will require an in-depth understanding of what the existing and targeted customers want, their specification and expectations and respond with new products that meet or exceed their needs. For example, after the dot-com bust, Amazon's stock price deflated, but the organization continued to grow as a result of refocusing their strategies on the customer. When an organization satisfies their customers, they are differentiating themselves from average performers and giving themselves greater opportunity for long-term growth and survival. By doing this, they are putting themselves in a stronger position to attract suppliers, customers, and stakeholders.

Summary

Innovation and entrepreneurial activity is achieved through people, individuals, and teams who are creative and innovative. Organizations need individuals who have the drive and motivation to be creative and innovative as well as the requisite skills and experience. In turn, the organization needs to nurture that drive and motivation by creating a work environment that reduces the obstacles and fosters the stimulants to creativity and innovation. Only then will the organization be poised to lead through innovation and entrepreneurship.

The entrepreneurial process and marketing activities need to be effectively integrated into the organization. MO supports the generation of knowledge in relation to customer needs that may allow an organization to incorporate such knowledge across a broader market of customers with the opportunity to increase their market share and enhance competitiveness. The alignment between EO and MO provides invaluable insights into how an organization can address market needs through their innovations. The alignment enables an organization to adapt and manage its market environment to satisfy the needs of existing and potential customers.

Learning contributes to the organization's innovation, entrepreneurship, and MO. EO extends the organization's scope for learning, particularly through opportunity identification and exploration. MO extends the organization's scope for learning—particularly through its focus on the market and the customer. Knowledge gained through learning can provide important information where there are significant gaps in the existing entrepreneurial and market activities. Innovative and entrepreneurial organizations are flexible, adaptable, and provide their people with the freedom and responsibility to utilize their creativity and champion innovative ideas.

Innovative and entrepreneurial activities that are market oriented and customer focused support and facilitate the organization's efforts to understand its customers' existing needs as well as their unmet needs. A comprehensive understanding of both market and customer needs are major sources of intelligence that facilitate opportunity recognition, innovation, and entrepreneurship within an organization.

There is a need to identify and exploit opportunities for innovation and entrepreneurship during challenging economic times in order to survive and grow. The pace and level of innovation inside the organization must be greater than outside for success, because there is increasing competitiveness in most markets and innovation is a KSF in most industry sectors. Successful organizations are characterized by focused, flexible, and fast innovations; these organizations seek synergy, alliances, and new ventures. Innovation and entrepreneurship is the key to growth, profitability, and sustained competitive advantage.

References

Covin, J. G., & Slevin, D. P. (1989). Strategic management of small firms in hostile and benign environments. *Strategic Management Journal, 10*, 75–87.

Miller, D. (1983). The correlates of entrepreneurship in three types of firms. *Management Science, 29*, 770–791.

Von Hippel, E. (1986). Lead users: A source of novel product concepts. *Management Science, 32*(7), 791–805.

Portions of this chapter adapted from Webb, J.W., Ireland, R. D., Hitt, M. A., Kistruck, G. M., Tihanyi, L. (2011). Where is the opportunity without the customer? An integration of marketing activities, the entrepreneurship process, and institutional theory. *Journal of the Academy of Marketing Science, 39*(4), 537–554.

Suggested Readings

Baker, W. E., & Sinkula, J. M. (2009). The complementary effects of market orientation and entrepreneurial orientation on profitability in small businesses. *Journal of Small Business Management, 47*(4), 443–464.

The results of this study suggest that EO and MO complement one another, at least in small businesses, to enhance profitability. The major difference between this and previous studies is the inclusion of innovation success, which captures an indirect effect of EO on profitability. Overall, the results suggest that EO complements MO in small firms by instilling an opportunistic culture that impacts the quality and quantity of firms' innovations.

Brockman, B. K., Jones, M. A., & Becherer, R. C. (2012). Customer orientation and performance in small firms: Examining the moderating influence of risk-taking, innovativeness, and opportunity focus. *Journal of Small Business Management, 50*(3), 429–446.

The authors examine the customer orientation–performance relationship among 180 small firms and the moderating influence of risk-taking, innovativeness, and opportunity focus on that relationship. Overall results support the positive influence of customer orientation on performance and indicate that the influence is stronger as risk-taking, innovativeness, and opportunity focus increase. However, their results also found that customer orientation did not positively influence small firm performance under low levels of risk-taking, innovativeness, and opportunity focus.

Covin, J. G., & Lumpkin, G. T. (2011). Entrepreneurial orientation theory and research: Reflections on a needed construct. *Entrepreneurship Theory and Practice, 35*(5), 855–872.

The authors in this article address substantive matters fundamental to the continuing development of EO theory and research including

(1) whether EO is more defensibly conceived as a dispositional or behavioral construct, (2) the reasons why some regard EO as an "annoying construct," (3) why EO fills an important gap in the literature on firm-level entrepreneurship, (4) proposal that EO proceed along two concurrent paths corresponding the unidimensional and multidimensional conceptualizations of the construct, (5) review of EO measurement issues, and (6) consideration of both marginal-value and high-potential topic areas for future EO theory and research.

Pérez-Luño, A., Wiklund, J., & Valle Cabrera, R. (2011). The dual nature of innovative activity: How entrepreneurial orientation influences innovation generation and adoption. *Journal of Business Venturing, 26*(5), 555–571.

The authors of this article analyze two modes of innovation that differ in their scope of newness: (1) innovation generation and (2) adoption. They developed a theoretical model based on the EO literature and utilized a unique sample of innovating firms. They found that 54% adopt innovations of other firms, 7% generate innovations internally, and 39% combine both. Additionally, their results show that proactivity and risk-taking influence the number of innovations generated and the extent to which firms favor generation over adoption and that environmental dynamism moderates one of these relationships.

Sirén, C., Kohtamaki, M., & Kuckertz, A. (2012). Exploration and exploitation strategies, profit performance and the mediating role of strategic learning: Escaping the exploitation trap. *Strategic Entrepreneurship Journal, 6*(1), 18–41.

The authors of this study focus on the role of strategic learning as a mediating construct between opportunity-seeking (exploration) and advantage-seeking (exploitation) strategies and profit performance. Results from 206 Finnish software firms found that strategic learning fully mediates the relationship among exploration, exploitation, and profit performance. Furthermore, the study demonstrates that the effect from exploration to strategic learning is moderated by the level of exploitation.

Tang, J., Kacmar, K. M., & Busenitz, L. (2012). Entrepreneurial alertness in the pursuit of new opportunities. *Journal of Business Venturing, 27*(1), 77–94.

The authors in this article provide a model involving three distinct elements of alertness: (1) scanning and search, (2) association and connection, and (3) evaluation and judgment. They conduct multiple studies to develop and validate a 13-item alertness scale that captures these three dimensions. Their instrument provides researchers with a valuable tool for probing the entrepreneurial opportunity development process including antecedents and outcomes.

Webb, J. W., Ireland, R. D., Hitt, M. A., Kistruck, G. M., & Tihanyi, L. (2011). Where is the opportunity without the customer? An integration of marketing activities, the entrepreneurship process, and institutional theory. *Journal of the Academy Marketing Science, 39*(4), 537–554.

In this article, the authors integrate research on marketing activities, the entrepreneurship process, and institutional theory in an effort to address how changes in the institutional environment may substantially alter the processes and outcomes of these undertakings. They discuss MO as enhancing a firm's opportunity recognition and innovation whereas marketing mix decisions enhance opportunity exploitation. They then examine how entrepreneurship leads to innovation directed toward MO and marketing mix activities. Based on this foundation, the authors examine differences in marketing and entrepreneurship activities across institutional contexts.

CHAPTER 6

Design Thinking and Innovation

W hat is design thinking? How can it be used to create significant innovation? Are there steps that can be followed to implement design thinking on an individual or company basis? Are there good examples of the successful use of design thinking in an organization?

Scenario: IKEA

Ingvar Kamprad was born in southern Sweden on March 30, 1926, and was raised on a farm called Elmtaryd near the small village of Agunnaryd. Even as a young boy, Kamprad had an entrepreneurial spirit. At the age of 5, he discovered a good profit could be made by buying matches cheaply in bulk in Stockholm and then individually reselling the matches to his neighbors in the country. He started by selling matches to his closest neighbors, but by the time he was 7, Kamprad put his growing match business on wheels, using his bicycle to sell matches to customers farther and farther from Elmtaryd. Gradually, Kamprad expanded his business offerings from selling only matches to also selling flower seeds, greeting cards, holiday decorations, pencils, and ballpoint pens.

In 1943, when Ingvar Kamprad completed school at the age of 17, his father gave him some money as a reward for doing well. Kamprad, the eternal entrepreneur, used this money to establish IKEA. The name IKEA was formed from his initials (*I* and *K*) and the first letters of Elmtaryd and Agunnaryd, the farm and village where he grew up. Initially, IKEA focused on the products Kamprad was already selling, but gradually the company expanded the product offerings to include wallets, watches, and jewelry. Within 2 short years, IKEA grew to such an extent that Kamprad could no longer make individual sales calls, and he launched a mail order service to continue meeting the growing customer demands for his products.

In 1948—just 5 years after starting IKEA—Kamprad introduced his first line of furniture using local manufacturers in the forests close to his home to supply the finished goods. The furniture line was a huge success, and Kamprad believed IKEA could become a large-scale furniture provider. In 1951, Kamprad decided to discontinue all other product lines in order to focus the company's attention solely on producing furniture. He launched the IKEA catalog strategy, which today remains one of IKEA's major advertising strategies. However, around this same time, IKEA became embroiled in a pricing war with its main competitor. As the two companies continued lowering prices, Kamprad became concerned about the quality of the furniture and the image customers would have of their quality. To address these concerns, in 1953 IKEA opened its initial furniture showroom to demonstrate the function and quality of IKEA's low-priced products. Located in Älmhult, Sweden, this first showroom was well received by customers because, for the first time, they could see the products in real life before purchasing them. The showroom concept worked, and it became a competitive differentiator with customers choosing IKEA over its competitors, leading to greater sales volumes.

In 1956, IKEA embarked on another mission that would change the company forever. In response to a supplier boycott organized by their competitors, IKEA began the process of vertically integrating their company by designing their own furniture. Coincidentally, around this same time, a local draughtsman realized that if he took the legs off an IKEA table, he could fit the table into the trunk of his car. Kamprad recognized the advantages of shipping furniture in such a way, and almost overnight, IKEA launched the flat pack model and revolutionized the company and the furniture industry. Going forward, IKEA designed furniture that could be shipped in flat packaging and assembled by customers after purchase, leading to easier transportation of furniture to customer homes as well as lower prices.

Throughout the next decade, IKEA expanded its stores from Sweden to neighboring countries including Denmark, Germany, and Switzerland. As increasing numbers of people showed up at IKEA showrooms, Kamprad decided to change the layout of the stores from that of a showroom to a self-service warehouse model that allowed customers to select and load their own furniture. This helped IKEA to further improve the customer experience and drive costs down even further. Wherever IKEA expanded to, it was successful in creating a cult-like following from its customers. IKEA opened its first store in the United States in 1985 and has grown today to be a global retail brand with over 131,000 employees. As of August 2011, the IKEA group operated 287 stores in 26 countries.

Kamprad's vision has been the driving force behind IKEA's continued success. In 1976, Kamprad wrote and published *The Testament of a Furniture Dealer,* documenting IKEA's vision and business idea, which had a strong influence on the development and vitality of IKEA's corporate culture. From inception, IKEA has been dedicated to meeting customer demands and providing them with high quality, well-functioning products at low prices. IKEA in its design thinking has intentionally kept product lines simple to minimize the potential for damage during transport and make it easier for customers to take their furniture home themselves. Kamprad believes his company exists not just to improve people's lives but to improve the people themselves ("Famous Entrepreneur Advice," n.d.). By allowing customers to select their furniture from the self-service warehouse store and to easily assemble their furniture at home, Kamprad believes he is improving customers' self-sufficiency and self-confidence. The vision of IKEA helping people to improve themselves is reinforced in IKEA's advertising and catalog.

Despite being one of the richest people in the world, Ingvar Kamprad also has a legendary reputation for thriftiness. He has always tried to set a good example for his employees by working hard and cutting costs wherever he can. He is the personification of the company he created and inherently understands that his workers look to him for direction. Kamprad's level of frugality is matched only by his desire to make the most of his time. One of his most important maxims that he outlines in his *The Testament of a Furniture Dealer* is that "most things still remain to be done." It is with the goals of efficiency and persistent work that the corporate philosophy of IKEA is built upon. An example of this is IKEA's focus on strictly maintaining a flat management structure within the organization.

Kamprad has repeatedly refused to take IKEA public, stating that it would slow the quick decision-making processes that allowed for IKEA's phenomenal growth. In 1982, Kamprad established IKEA Group and gave his shares to Stitching INGKA Foundation, a charity supporting "innovation in the field of architecture and interior" ("IKEA: Flat-Pack Accounting," 2006). Kamprad made this move for the express objective of avoiding high taxes in Sweden and to ensure the company he worked so hard to build could not be ruined or sold by future members of the Kamprad family. In 1986, Kamprad retired from the CEO position and has since taken up an advisory role to the holding company.

Through working hard, having a keen ability to turn obstacles into competitive advantages, and encouraging what is now labeled as Design Thinking, Kamprad successfully built one of the largest and most profitable companies in history and distinguished himself as one of the most savvy and successful entrepreneurs of our time. Although his career has not been without its share of controversy, Kamprad has always owned up to his mistakes and is famous for saying, "Only those who are asleep make no mistakes" ("SUCCESS Quotes by Legendary Billionaires," n.d.).

Definition of Design Thinking

Design thinking is a new approach to create breakthrough innovation and promote high-performance collaboration. It is quite different from analytical thinking and is a process for action. It is a method for discovering new opportunities and solving problems. While there are a variety of techniques and tools that can be used, the core process is somewhat universal.

Aspects of Design Thinking

It is generally understood that there are five key elements in design thinking: (1) defining the problem, (2) developing the options, (3) determining the direction, (4) selecting the best solution, and (5) executing. The steps have some degree of similarity to those in the scientific process. Each of these will be discussed in turn.

Defining the Problem

This first step, correctly defining the problem, while sounding simple is often the most difficult of design thinking. If the right problem is not defined, then of course the solution, if obtained, is for something else. Defining the problem is usually a team effort with a significant amount of participation by each team member.

Defining the problem usually involves observation—discerning what individuals actually do versus what they may say they do. It also involves cross-functional thinking trying to find the real issues involved. Any preconceived notions or judgments need to be abandoned so that the right problem can be defined in such a way that creative solutions can occur. If the problem is a sitting apparatus, the problem is not to design a chair but to design something to suspend a person from the floor.

Developing the Options

Once the problem is defined, the second element—developing the options—takes place. Care should be taken not to take the same approach as has been used in the past. Design thinking requires the creation of several solutions to the problem for consideration even when one solution seems obvious. For this to occur, multiple perspectives and team involvement are important. Multiple people involved develop a far richer range of solutions.

Determining the Direction

This third stage—determining the direction—requires that the most promising solutions are carefully nurtured. An environment in the organization needs to be created so that each solution can be allowed to develop and grow. This environment of experimentation and testing allows the best solution to emerge. Often during this stage, ideas are combined to form an even better solution.

Selecting the Best Solution

From the many solutions maturing from the previous stage, the best solution can be selected. Prototypes of this solution are created and tested. This vigorous testing helps to ensure that the final solution is the best possible one.

Executing

Once the optimal form of the solution to the problem is found, the solution needs to be implemented. This execution element may prove difficult particularly when significant change is involved. Design thinking involves the acceptance of change and risk, which is often not easily embraced both by individuals and organizations. Execution also involves implementing design thinking on a continual basis as it is a repeatable process that will result in creative solutions to problems defined.

Organizational Barriers

Even when the best methodology and techniques are employed, for design thinking to succeed, there is a need for organizational commitment. When first understanding design thinking, an organization should be prepared to fail at the beginning. Most people find it difficult to use their imaginations and react to distractions. In design thinking, failure is not necessarily bad as it can often lead to success. Design thinking focuses on and nurtures a number of alternatives until the best solution emerges. Some common organization issues develop the following barriers to the successful implementation of design thinking.

Lack of Management Commitment

This barrier is a significant one that occurs in organizations. Top-level management must openly endorse and practice design thinking. Without this, employees at lower levels of the organization will not embrace and practice it themselves. In many cases, there is resistance at some level in the organization. This *permafrost* or resistance to using design thinking needs to be unfrozen through training and education. In some cases, the only method of removal is eliminating or reassigning the source of the permafrost.

Lack of Performance Indicators

Another barrier to the successful use of design thinking is due to the lack of measureable indicators of success. The lack of a quantifiable framework to measure the output of design thinking makes it difficult for some organizations to accept and implement it as a problem solving methodology. In some organizations, it is important to begin design thinking by focusing on a small problem with a significant upside potential.

Resistance to Change

As with anything new, people and organizations are resistant to change even when they think it is a good thing. This is particularly the case when it causes discomfort and a change in behavior. The more radical the change in behavior that is required in an organization to adopt design thinking, the more the resistance to this change will occur. When this is the case, it is often easier to start the first design thinking process on a problem that is totally outside the usual domain. Once individuals become familiar with the technique, it can then be used to focus on solutions to problems in their usual domain. Three companies will be discussed that have overcome these and other organizational barriers and successfully implemented design thinking: (1) IDEO, (2) Redbox Automated Retail LLC, and (3) IKEA.

Table 6.1 Characteristics of a Design-Thinking Organization

- Supports people
- Protects people
- Tolerates mistakes
- Advises people
- Takes risks
- Shares a vision
- Delegates to those closest to the problem
- Tolerates internal competition
- Stimulates creativity
- Actively searches for ideas
- Tolerates disorder
- Encourages experimentation and tests
- Trusts people
- Tolerates ambiguity
- Does not interfere

Overall Culture

The overall culture of the organization can either support or inhibit design thinking. An organizational culture that is guided by a vision, encourages freedom, and has such characteristics as trust, belief in people, expandability, people growth, and job ownership allows more creativity to occur and increases the quality and output of design thinking versus a more traditional organizational culture. This type of organization provides an environment for employees to want to own their jobs and do everything possible to make the organization and the results of their position world class. A list of the characteristics of this type of organization is found in Table 6.1. The overall cultural climate is one of sharing, trying something new, suggesting and experimenting, and feeling responsible.

IDEO

The company that is probably most well known for successfully implementing design thinking to solve problems in a variety of company situations is IDEO. These applications include designing the Pilates Allegro 2 Reformer, building the ultimate utility bicycle, designing Walgreens' community pharmacy, designing the Steelcase node chair, developing Gannett Company's bold italic, designing Changi General Hospital's orthopedic clinic patient experience, and designing the ideal home for the Wounded Warriors.

In one project for Bank of America, IDEO worked with a team from the bank focused on the consumer behavior of putting their change received in a jar at home. Once the jar is full, it is either spent on something special or else deposited in a bank account. To mirror this behavior, in 2005, Bank of America launched a new savings account service called "Keep the Change." Customers who apply for and use their new debit card to make purchases can round up the purchase to the nearest dollar and have the difference deposited directly in their savings account. While this design thinking output encourages people to save, appealing to each individual's instinctive desire to put money aside in a painless way, the real payoff is an emotional one—seeing an increase in the monthly savings account statement without much effort.

IDEO also used design thinking with a team from Kaiser Permanente, a large health care provider. Kaiser wanted all of its administrators, doctors, and nurses to use design thinking in providing solutions to problems encountered and inspire new ideas. One project was to reengineer nursing shift changes at several Kaiser hospitals. The team from IDEO and the hospital working with frontline practitioners from each hospital first identified the problems occurring during shift changes. Potential solutions were explored through brainstorming and service prototyping. The options were evaluated to determine the best solution to shift changing, which was then implemented.

Besides services, IDEO has worked on a variety of products in the health care area. When a group of surgeons were describing the ideal product for sinus surgery and all its characteristics and features, the team from IDEO created some initial designs and prototypes. These were then tested and evaluated and a final prototype was developed, which was followed by the final product for sinus surgery. These examples of IDEO using design thinking show the one basic rule for success: Keep as many options in play as long as possible so that the best possible solution can emerge.

Redbox Automated Retail, LLC

Redbox Automated Retail, LLC, a wholly owned subsidiary of Coinstar, Inc., provides Blu-ray discs, newly released DVDs, and/or video games for rent through conveniently located kiosks. The over 35,400 kiosks, designed with the assistance of IDEO, are located in places where individuals shop, making renting and returning a convenient, simple, timely process. The new self-service kiosk, developed through the design thinking process, enhances the consumer experience in making an average $2 rental by moving them through stages in the decision process: attract, educate, and engage. The layered signage attracts the consumers to the red box where they can browse (educate) through the changing titles and easily make the purchase decision (engage).

The new kiosks are in locations throughout the United States inside and outside of leading grocery, drug, and convenience stores such as Walgreens and Walmart as well as fast-food franchises such as McDonald's. Redbox contributed to the increased market share in this rental market from kiosks and achieved its 2 billionth rental at a McDonald's restaurant in Philomath, Oregon. The company feels the new kiosk created through the design thinking process contributed significantly to its success and growth.

IKEA

The company appropriately featured as the scenario to this chapter, IKEA, is a great example of the design thinking process. As stated earlier, IKEA was founded in 1943 in a small village (Agunnaryd) in Sweden; their vision is to create a better everyday life through modern yet not trendy home furnishings. The vision transferred into a wide range of uniquely designed home furnishing products that are very functional in nature. Each product reflects the Swedish approach to design thinking. Each is attractive yet functional, human-oriented, and environmentally friendly. The unique design thinking apparent in each home furnishing product represents the healthy, fresh Swedish lifestyle. The carefully chosen colors and materials are part of this design thinking allowing IKEA to be a major retail player in over 45 countries. By maximizing the functionality, use of raw materials, and efficient production, IKEA can meet the needs and desires of the market at a low cost. This low cost and resulting lower retail price allows the home furnishings to appeal to a broad market.

IKEA's vision is evident in its outreach and promotional efforts. In 2011, the company launched Share Space—a community photo-sharing website where individuals can share photos using IKEA products in their own living spaces. Customers are encouraged to share their own design thinking by sharing their personal solutions to design challenges in their living rooms, kitchens, or other areas in the home. One room will be selected by IKEA design experts as the "Pick of the Week" and is then featured on the Share Space homepage and in the company's blog.

Another unique project is the Life Improvement Project (LIP) to inspire consumers to create a better life for themselves. This program communicates the brand and the vision of the company. One feature of the LIP is the Life Improvement Sabbatical contest. The winner receives one year off from work and $100,000 to advance any project that improves the lives of others.

Future

As is evident in each of these examples as well as in many organizations around the world, design thinking has provided many benefits and interesting results. Through this new process format, design thinking allowed organizations to expand their ideas and offerings resulting in many successes but also many failures. Some organizations turned the process into a linear step-by-step methodology that often delivered nothing creative and at best incremental change and innovation. While design thinking will of course continue to be used with mixed results in the future, two other approaches also offer a way to switch between multiple perspectives and institute creativity—(1) futures thinking and creative intelligence (CQ).

Futures Thinking

Futures thinking combines data, trend analysis, intuition, and imagination to develop sustainable paths of action. It is a set of practices and principles for solving problems regardless of their degree of complexity. It consists basically of four aspects: (1) asking the question, (2) scanning the world, (3) mapping the possibilities, and (4) asking the next question. Like design thinking, futures thinking is an iterative process to consider a range of possibilities and outcomes. This new way of thinking is based on practical research and analysis in challenging assumptions about the problem and its most favorable solution.

Creative Intelligence

Since one of the major objectives of design thinking was to stimulate creativity, this is the prime focus of CQ, framing problems in new ways in order to develop original solutions. It is more of a sociological approach with creativity emerging from group activity. CQ is a hybrid of design thinking, scenario planning, systems thinking, and gaming.

References

Famous entrepreneur advice. (n.d.). Retrieved March 17, 2013, from www.evancar michael.com/Famous-Entrepreneurs/825/summary.php

IKEA: Flat-pack accounting. (2006, May 11). *The Economist, 379*(8477), 76.

Kamprad, I. (1976). *The testament of a furniture dealer: A little IKEA dictionary.* Netherlands: Inter IKEA Systems B.V.

SUCCESS quotes by legendary billionaires. (n.d.). Retrieved March 17, 2013, from www.mycomeup.com/Success-Quotes/SUCCESS-Quotes-By-Legendary-Billionaires-Updated-Version.html

Suggested Readings

Fraser, H. (2006, Spring/Summer). Turning design thinking into design doing. *Rotman Magazine*, 24–28.

In this article, Heather Fraser, director of Business Design Initiatives in the Desautels Centre for Integrative Thinking at the Rotman School, exposes the different lessons on how best to transform "inspiration into implementation." If design is now considered a business necessity for competitive edge, it is crucial for business leaders to understand how to truly convert design into "an accessible, doable program." The author argues that design thinking is far from being "an attribute"; it is fundamentally about action.

Mootee, I. (2011, March). Strategic innovation and the fuzzy front end. *Ivey Business Journal, 21*, 38–42.

The author presents the design thinking process under a new light that he refers to as "the fuzzy front end." Idris Mootee advocates this new approach as a critical and systematic process that companies should incorporate to their management mind-set for getting a better picture of the future and identifying opportunities that otherwise would be missed. Throughout the article, the author presents the fuzzy front-end approach as an "insight-driven, prototype-powered and foresight-inspired search for new ideas that can be applied to products, services, experiences, business strategies, and business models" (p. 38).

Tischler, L. (2011, October). The United States of design. *Fast Company, 159*, 77–88.

Linda Tischler presents a series of new and existing U.S. businesses that successfully combine innovation, design, and technology in their management and product offerings. The article posits that now that American firms have made customers their pivotal point of focus, American design is having a global impact in everything from fashion to human/machine interface, system design, and health care devices. Design worldwide is also discussed as more and more countries are also investing in design and integrating it into their business models.

SECTION 3

OPERATIONALIZING INNOVATION AND ENTREPRENEURSHIP

CHAPTER 7

Developing New Products, Services, and Ventures

W hy is it important for an organization to continuously develop new products and/or services? What are some techniques for doing this successfully? What are the successes and pitfalls? How can this result in the creation of a new venture? Are there ways to develop innovations outside the existing strategy of the organization?

Scenario: Reliance India

Dhirubhai Ambani was born into a family of modest means on December 28, 1932, in Gujarat, India. At the age of 16, after completing high school, Ambani moved to Aden, Yemen, and worked as a dispatch clerk for A. Besse & Co., a transcontinental trading firm. Two years later when A. Besse & Co. became the primary distributor for Shell Oil, Ambani was promoted to manage the company's oil-filling station at the Port of Aden. At the time, Aden was the largest trading port in the world with goods coming from and being dispatched to every continent. Throughout the Aden bazaars, speculation of manufactured goods and commodities was common. To learn the tricks of the trade, Ambani spent his spare time working for free for a local trading firm learning accounting, bookkeeping, and the inner workings of the shipping industry, including preparing shipping documents and negotiating with banks and insurance companies. These skills were crucial 10 years later when he started his own trading company in Mumbai, India. After learning the basics of commodities trading, Ambani began speculating in the purchase and sale of various goods. Initially, unable to fund the speculative trading himself, Ambani borrowed money from friends and small Aden shopkeepers on the terms that "profit we share and all loss will be mine." It was very quickly clear that Ambani had an uncanny knack for speculative trading and rarely lost money in any deal. One example of Ambani's speculative skills occurred in the 1950s when the Yemini administration realized that their main unit of currency, the rial, was quickly disappearing. Upon investigating, the administration realized that significant quantities of rials were being routed to a man in his 20s in the Port City of Aden. There they found Dhirubhai Ambani, who was buying unlimited amounts of Yemini rials, which were made of pure silver, melting them down and making a healthy profit selling the silver to bullion traders in London where silver was in high demand. Even at a young age, Ambani's keen ability to identify and capitalize on opportunities was unsurpassed.

In 1958, Ambani left Yemen and returned to India to set up a textile trading company, Reliance Commercial Corp, with his cousin. The trading company imported polyester yarn and exported spices to Yemen. This was during the era of India's infamous "license-permit raj," when local businessmen with political connections could obtain exclusive rights to export, import, and manufacture licenses and then over time accumulate huge fortunes. Ambani foresaw a time when Indians with higher disposable incomes would buy better quality, more expensive clothing. In order to meet this forthcoming demand, Ambani obtained the necessary clearances to manufacture clothing from polyester fiber and opened his first textile mill in 1966 in the small town of Naroda, India. With the trading company operating smoothly, Ambani concentrated on quietly building his new clothing business under the brand name Vimal. By extensively marketing the Vimal brand, Ambani was soon able to turn the Vimal brand into a household name. To get around the reluctance of established wholesalers and shopkeepers to sell the company's products, Ambani opened his own network of over 400 franchised shops across India to sell the Vimal brand of polyester materials for saris, shirts, suits, and dresses. In 1975, a technical team from the World Bank visited Reliance's textile manufacturing facilities and awarded the company with the rare distinction of being certified as "excellent even by developed country standards" during that period.

Though Reliance was profitable, Ambani quickly realized that to continue future growth and expansion, especially into unrelated sectors, he would need to obtain access to cheap sources of capital. Rather than pursuing traditional methods of funding from the banking system, he decided to tap Mumbai's infant stock market exchange. In Reliance's 1977 initial public offering (IPO), the company was able to raise adequate funds with more than 58,000 investors buying shares. After the positive response to the IPO, Reliance continued over the years to sell shares to fund various growth and expansion initiatives. Over time, the number of Reliance shareholders gradually climbed to over 3 million people. In order to accommodate this large number of shareholders, Reliance now conducts annual shareholder meetings in large sports stadiums in India. As the company grew, Ambani also became a local hero and was regarded by shareholders with admiration and even reverence.

After raising the necessary capital in 1982, Ambani began the process of vertically integrating operations by setting up a plant to manufacture polyester filament yarn. He subsequently diversified his company further and entered into chemical, gas, petrochemical, plastics, energy, and telecom services. By the late 1980s, Reliance was one of India's most powerful and profitable business entities. However, the phenomenal growth of Reliance owed much to Ambani's business acumen and ability to get India's rules and regulations, including import tariffs introduced, changed, or removed in order to create competitive advantages for Reliance—many times at the expense of his Indian competitors. His methods of creating competitive advantages at the expense of others earned him many enemies in India's competitive corporate world. Ambani nevertheless forged ahead, cultivating friendships in almost every political party in India and managing media relations in such a way that any stories about Reliance's questionable business approaches seldom made it into the mainstream media.

Reliance's vertical integration strategy meant that the company wanted to extend its operations to include petroleum refining, exploration and production. But during the 1976 global oil crisis, the Indian oil industry had been nationalized, and these sectors were state-owned entities. By the early 1990s, however, the state-owned oil companies were unable to meet demand and were facing a liquidity crisis. During this time in 1993, Reliance Petroleum Limited was established. The company immediately began developing petroleum products and distribution operations, including a network of over 1,000 fueling stations. The money needed for this subsidiary was raised through India's first foreign market placement through a global depositary receipt (GDR) issued in Luxembourg.

Reliance was able to enter into the refinery business in 1997 when the Indian oil industry was also faced with a liquidity crisis causing the government to open up the sector. In response, Reliance gained government approval for and started building one of the largest and most modern petroleum refining plants in the world. The plant was located in Jamnagar, Gujarat (India), and cost an estimated USD $6 billion to build. Completed in 1999, the plant was built in record time, and upon opening, it ranked as one of the top five refineries in the world for production capacity. The building of the refining facility catapulted Reliance to the top of India's private-sector companies, and Reliance became the first Indian company to be featured on the Forbes 500 list.

Combining smart business sense with a keen ability to navigate through Indian politics, Ambani rose from modest origins to single-handedly building the largest private-sector company in India that, in 30 years' time, outgrew other corporate giants in India such as Tata and Birla, which had dominated the private sector for nearly a century. At the time of Ambani's death in 2002, Reliance Group had revenues of USD $15 billion. One of Ambani's famous quotes was this:

> I have trusted people, and they have put their trust in me. I have encouraged youth, and they have never let me down. I have asked my people to take initiative and to take risks. It has paid me rich dividends. I insist on excellence. This helps us to be leaders. Reliance is built on some of these principles.

In 2000, the Federation of Indian Chambers of Commerce and Industry (FICCI) named Dhirubhai Ambani the "Indian Entrepreneur of the 20th Century." Also in 2000, *The Times of India* voted him "greatest creator of wealth in the century." Most people will agree that Ambani had a vision and business acumen that was unmatched. In one of his more candid moments, the otherwise reticent tycoon summed up the secret of his remarkable success story: "Think big, think fast and think ahead. Ideas are no one's monopoly."

Reliance has continued to grow and evolve as a company through continuously adding new products and services.

SOURCE: Adapted from www.dhirubhai.net/dhapp/home.jsp; www.ril.com, www.referenceforbusiness.com/history2/78/Reliance-Industries-Ltd.html#ixzz1rhXO2kk3; and Joseph's *Eq and Leadership,* Pages 314-317. Tata McGraw-Hill Publishing Ltd. New Delhi: 2007

Introduction

As occurs in Reliance Industries, there are several aspects of developing successful new products and services. The first aspect is, of course, determining available opportunities. This can be done through market assessment and using the trimming technique. These ideas then need to be screened, which can be done through use of the product planning and development process, the idea development process, and the opportunity assessment plan. Regardless of the screening process employed, the concept of newness to the organization and consumer and distribution system needs to be taken into account.

Determining Available Opportunities

While there are several ways to determine some market opportunities, two that the authors have found very useful—particularly for companies and more technology-oriented individuals—are market assessment through gap analysis and the trimming technique.

Gap Analysis

Gap analysis is a useful technique for identifying market areas where no products or services exist. It can include looking at product line gaps, distribution gaps, usage gaps, and a gap where no competitive products/services exist. The latter one, which involves the creation of a new unique product, has the highest potential for a successful sustainable launch and usually results from understanding a need in the market, which presently is not being totally fulfilled.

Gap analysis can also focus on products, prices, distribution, and usage. Probably the most frequently used is product gap analysis. This involves evaluating the various products that fill a market need to see if there are any gaps in such areas as size, options, style, color, flavor, fragrance, or form (method of operation, range of operation, product format, or product composition). Sometimes developing a new package—perhaps one that is reusable or environmentally friendly or can be used for another purpose—creates an entirely different product/packaging market opportunity. One company created a unique packaging system for milk that allowed large discount stores like Costco, Walmart, and Sam's Club to save money in storing, displaying, and selling milk products.

Closely related to product gap analysis is price gap analysis. There are often gaps in prices in a product line or products in different locations that provide a market opportunity. One company created Dr. John's toothbrush, the first low cost battery powered toothbrush, to fill the gap between low priced manual toothbrushes and higher priced powered toothbrushes. The company was bought by Procter & Gamble (P&G), and the product was the basis of the Crest toothbrush available today. Other price gaps occur in different parts of a country sometimes reflecting a lack of communication, amount of sales, or other costs. This price difference may allow a new product to be introduced in related regional markets with the higher prices.

Distribution gaps, a third area for focus, can occur in terms of coverage, intensity, or exposure. Sometimes a different type of product than the one selling in upscale stores, such as Macy's, can be successfully sold in discount stores. An available market may be a distribution system that requires a lower number of products (intensity) than is the standard shipping order or one that is difficult to reach (intensity). One product was successful being sold through cruise ships and gift shops at resorts that cater to tourists.

The final gap is in usage. This can take the form of nonusers, light users, or light usage. Trying to increase the usage among current users is reflected in many commercials where the product (such as orange juice) is not first for consumption in a certain period of time (breakfast in the morning). Of these, connecting nonusers is the most difficult— particularly if these nonusers once used the product.

Trimming Technique

The trimming technique is a unique way to systematically explore the rigorous aspects, components, and functions of an innovation trying to reduce or eliminate some to develop new ideas. These can be done through applying some of the following rules:

- Recipient can perform the function itself
- Recipient of the function can be eliminated
- Function does not need to exist
- Function can be performed by some other part of the larger system
- Function can be better performed by a new or improved part
- A new mark can be identified for the newly trimmed product

In looking at an existing product or a new innovation, one or more of the rules applicable should be used. For example, applying the rules that a function does not need to exist and the rule that the function can be performed by some other part of the larger system to the stem of a wine glass, Riedel developed stemless wine glasses. The new form of wine glass maintains classic slopes to enhance the flavor of the wine. The new stemless glass is easier to store and fits better in the dishwasher.

The same rules as well as the rule that the function can be performed by a new or improved part were applied to the stem of a wine glass and its composition of glass. Govino developed stemless wine glasses made from a flexible, BPA-free odorless polymer. The material reflects the color of the wine and projects the aroma much like crystal. Since it is not breakable, this wine glass can be used in settings where breakable glass cannot be used. The company added a nice touch—an ergonomic thumb notch on the side to provide a clean, comfortable grip.

Using another example of toilet paper and the rule that the recipient of the function can perform the function itself, the cardboard roll in the toilet paper can be removed (trimmed), letting the role of paper perform the function itself.

Applying the rule that the function does not need to exist and the rule that the function can be better performed by a new, improved part to an older module of a tape recorder by Sony produced the Walkman with memory and no tapes as well as many other new versions of a tape recorder. Similarly, IBM trimmed the speakers and sent a high frequency current to the motor to make it resonate different tones in its Pro Printer. Also, Cirque de Soleil trimmed the animal acts in order to add theatrical content.

As is illustrated in these examples, the rules of the trimming technique are great ways to decompose an innovation (or an existing product) and look at its various components and functions.

Product Planning and Development Process

A standardized approach for developing new products and services is the product planning and development process. As indicated in Figure 7.1, this process consists of four stages with an evaluation being done at the end of each stage—(1) idea stage, (2) concept stage, (3) product development stage, and (4) test marketing stage. To work effectively, evaluation criteria need to be established and employed at each stage that either rejects an innovation or allows it to proceed to the next stage.

The first stage, the idea stage, is when the innovation is formulated and developed. There are many ways these innovative ideas occur. Sometimes the innovation comes from observing trends. There are several trends occurring today that will provide the opportunity for new innovations. These include the organic food trend, the green trend, the health trend, the clean energy trend, and the social media trend. Just look at the increasing aging of the population around the world or the number of people tweeting, and you can see the trends and their increasing size. Other sources of innovative ideas include assessing the inventor's own research, evaluating existing products and services in the marketplace, listening to the consumers' complaints and suggestions, and observing new legal requirements to doing business in a country. Regardless of the innovation, it needs to be evaluated at this stage by applying the evaluation criteria established to determine if the product/service should move on to the next stage.

Figure 7.1 The Product Planning and Development Process

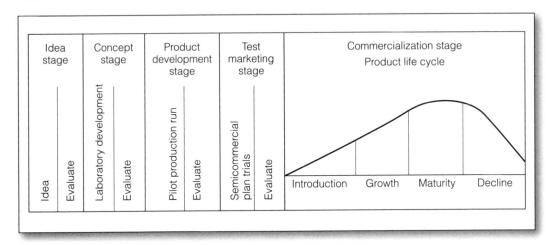

SOURCE: Hisrich, Robert, *Marketing Decisions for New and Mature* Products, 2nd ed., ©1991. Printed and Electronically reproduced by permission of Pearson Education, Inc., Upper Saddle River, New Jersey.

After the innovation has passed the evaluation process in the idea stage, it moves to the concept stage. In this stage, the modified innovation is tested to determine market reaction and the degree of acceptance. While various methods can be employed, one of the easiest, cost effective methods is to discuss the innovation with individuals in the defined market. This is called a conversational interview. Various features, price, and promotional aspects of the innovation should be discussed in comparison to competitive products/services available in the market—particularly the ones presently being used to fulfill the market need. Again, the information needs to be analyzed using the evaluation criteria established before passing on to the next stage—the product development stage.

In the product development stage, a final version of the product based in part on the evaluations obtained in the concept stage for further consumer input. Again, consumer feedback is obtained, and the refined innovation is evaluated against the evaluation criteria established.

Following a successful evaluation, the innovation moves into the final stage before finally being evaluated and launched, which is the start of the product life cycle (see Figure 7.1). In this, the test marketing stage, a market test of the innovation is done to help ensure successful commercialization. Due to the costs of test markets and the nature of some products/services, this stage is often bypassed with the innovation going from the product development stage direct to commercialization.

Figure 7.2 Idea Development Process

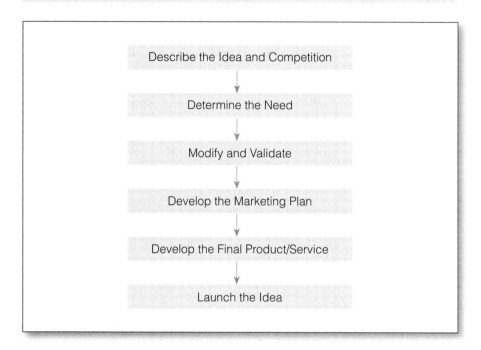

Idea Development Process

The idea process is a process that results in developing successful sustainable innovative new ideas. It is composed of six stages as shown in Figure 7.2.

As is indicated, the first stage is to describe the idea; evaluate any products/services that are filling the same need; and determine the advantages, benefits, and features that provide these benefits of your idea. While this is further discussed in the Opportunity Assessment Plan section at the end of the chapter, it is important to describe as succinctly as possible the details of the idea, the problem it solves, and the need it fills. The country system code that best describes the product should be determined. For example, this is the NAICS (North American Industry Classification System) code in the United States and the SIC (Standard Industrial Classification) code in China and Korea. This code can help you identify competitive products/services and their prices. This will allow the determination of the unique features of your innovation (compared to the competitive ones presently on the market filling the same need) and the features that deliver each of those benefits.

The second stage is to determine the need for your innovation. This requires as in-depth description as possible in stage one. Three different groups of consumers or firms should be identified that might benefit from your innovation with a customer profile for each group established. For business-to-consumer (B2C) groups, this profile should include at the minimum age range, income range, and gender. Family size, education, occupation, and race are helpful but not as critical. For business-to-business (B2B) groups, the profile should include industry, type of products/ services, location, and size. A concept survey instrument should be developed that includes a brief description including, where applicable, a diagram of your innovation and the survey questions that need to be asked. The results of the concept survey of members of each of the three groups should be analyzed to indicate the important criteria that interest your potential customers.

Modify and validate, the third stage, involves developing a prototype template of your innovation and interviewing individuals concerning this prototype. The questions concerning the prototype should focus on features and benefits of your prototype, the important aspects of this particular product, and the buying process involved.

Stage four involves developing a detailed marketing plan. The marketing plan, which is further discussed in the next chapter—Chapter 8 on the business plan—focuses on pricing, distribution, and communication (promotion). The pricing data obtained in your competitive analysis (stage one) should be evaluated along with the cost data to determine an initial price. The distribution plan involves determining the geographic area where your innovation will be sold and how you will physically get it there along with the distribution channel(s), when applicable. Finally, all the possible marketing communication tools appropriate should be considered, including the importance of social media.

The development of the actual idea is the fifth stage. This involves the development of the features of the final idea, its marketing theme, naming, and packaging (if appropriate). The marketing theme needs to focus on your key benefits or unique selling propositions that appeal to your target customers. The package, when appropriate, has many aspects, the most important of which is eye appeal when using a retail distribution.

The sixth and final stage is to launch the final product or service. This starts the product life cycle, which was previously discussed (see Figure 7.1).

Concept of Newness

One of the critical concepts affecting the successful launch and sustainability of an innovation is its newness. While, of course, newness or uniqueness is needed and in fact is an essential part of an innovation. Yet this same degree of newness affects the acceptability and the length of the adoption cycle for consumers, the individual investor and/or the organization, and the distribution system.

Newness to Consumer

Regardless of whether the innovation is for the consumer market (B2C) or the industrial market (B2B), if it is too far in advance of where the market is in terms of the market area, problems can occur. It is best to view the newness of the innovation in terms of its disruption on the established consumption patterns or lifestyles of the target market. The least disruptive innovations—continuous innovations—have little impact or influence on the lifestyle of the purchaser and therefore usually do not take as long in the evaluation and adoption stage. The majority of innovations are in this category.

A single focus on a particular item in a restaurant chain is an example of a continuous innovation. While it is important for the innovative item of focus to have a broad enough appeal and versatility to be the main feature on the menu, the item itself can vary from eggs to soups to chicken to roast beef. The Another Broken Egg Café, an upmarket brunch restaurant, focuses on the preparation of eggs in various ways and now has 20 units and about 150 items on the menu. Original Soup Man has 16 locations featuring between 6 and 12 varieties of soups daily with staples such as lobster bisque and Mexican bean soup along with different sandwich selections. Kentucky Fried Chicken is an internationally-oriented chain focusing on chicken. And Arby's focuses on roast beef sandwiches.

The concept needs to be broad enough and appealing as a main item preferably in at least two meal times. This was not the case for PB Loco, a gourmet peanut butter and jelly chain that, in 2005, started franchising. While initially heralded for its unique flavor combinations, the concept did not have appeal for breakfast and dinner and was considered an occasional novelty item, not a constant regular eating experience.

Newness to Individual and Organization

The newness of the innovation to the individual and, where appropriate, the organization is also important to access. The first time an individual invents, or even the first time an innovation is in a new area, there are more difficulties in developing and launching the innovation. This is reflected in the rule that most venture capitalists use—that someone on the management team, if not the entrepreneur, has experience in the industry of the new venture.

Similarly, when an innovation for an organization has both technological newness and market newness, it is viewed as diversification (see Figure 7.3). This situation versus all the others indicated on either the technology or market newness axis causes the highest level of problems and even failures for companies regardless of size. This is evidenced from

Figure 7.3 New Product Classification System

Market Newness / Technology Newness →

Product Objectives	No Technological Change	Improved Technology	New Technology
No market change		**Reformation** Change in formula or physical product to optimize costs and quality	**Replacement** Replace existing product with new one based on improved technology
Strengthened market	**Remerchandising** Increase sales to existing customers	**Improved product** Improved product's utility to customers	**Product life extension** Add new similar products to line; serve more customers based on new technology
New market	**New use** Add new segments that can use present products	**Market extension** Add new segments modifying present products	**Diversification** Add new markets with new products developed from new technology

SOURCE: Hisrich, R., Peters, M., & Shepherd, D. (2012). *Entrepreneurship* (9th ed.). New York: McGraw-Hill.

the failure of the Gillette LCD watch, which was well outside the parameters of the typical products of the company.

Newness to the Distribution System

The final area of concern is newness to the distribution system. Like consumers, individuals, and organizations, distribution systems have lifestyles—ways of doing things. An innovation outside its typical product category, size, shelf fit, or packaging will have a more difficult time gaining access. A new dog treat that was odorless to humans but loved by dogs could not access the retail stores in the United States until a new package size and design was developed, allowing the dog treat to be displayed on the shelves set aside for this type of product.

Opportunity Assessment Plan

Probably one of the best methods to use to ascertain the marketability of an innovation is the opportunity assessment plan. The opportunity assessment plan compared to a business plan (discussed in Chapter 8) is shorter; focused on the opportunity and market not a business; and has no financial plan, marketing plan, or organizational plan. It is used to determine if the innovation has at least three to five unique features (unique selling propositions) compared to the competitive product/service presently on the market filling the same need and has a market that is large enough, growing and accessible to warrant pursuing the innovation.

As is indicated in Table 7.1, it has four sections—two major and two minor sections. Section 1, a major section, focuses on the product/service idea and the competition. It requires obtaining the country system code of the country such as NAICS for the United States and SIC for China and Korea. After defining the innovation as thoroughly as possible, the various aspects of the product/service filling the need are obtained indicating the innovation's unique selling propositions.

The second section—another major section—focuses on the market for the innovation. Numbers over the past 3 to 5 years should be obtained on the size of this market so that a trend is obtained. The growth rate of the market should also be obtained. An innovation has a much stronger chance of success in a large, growing market than one that has leveled or is declining.

Sections 3 and 4—minor sections—focus respectively on the skills, experience, and background of the team and the steps needed to launch the innovation (see Table 7.1). Section 4 is particularly important as it gives an indication of the time and money needed for successfully developing and launching the innovation.

Table 7.1 Opportunity Assessment Plan

An opportunity assessment plan is NOT a business plan. Compared to a business plan, it should:

- Be shorter
- Focus on the opportunity, not the venture
- Have no computer-based spreadsheet
- Be the basis to make the decision on whether to act on an opportunity or wait until another, better opportunity comes along

Section 1

A description of the product or service

- What is the market need for the product or service?
- What are the specific aspects of the product or service (include any copyright, patent or trademark information)?
- What competitive products are available filling this need?
- What are the competitive companies in this product market space and their strengths and weaknesses?
- What are the country counting codes for this product or service?
- What are the unique selling propositions of this product or service?

Section 2

An assessment of the opportunity:

- What market need does it fill?
- What is the size and past trends of this market?
- What is the future growth and characteristics of this market?
- What are total industry sales over the past 5 years?
- What is anticipated growth in this industry?
- What is the profile of your typical customers?

Section 3

Entrepreneurial self-assessment and the entrepreneurial team:

- Why does this opportunity interest you?
- What are your reasons for going into business?
- How does it fit into your background and experience?
- What experience is needed to successfully launch the product/service?

Section 4

What needs to be done to translate this opportunity into a viable venture?

- Establish each critical step in order
- Determine the time and money needed at each step
- Determine the total amount of money needed and its source

Summary

This chapter focused on the importance of continuously developing new products/services. As occurs regularly in Reliance India, innovation needs to be continuously stressed in every organization. Processes such as gap analysis, trimming techniques, and the product planning and development process need to be instituted to develop and evaluate new ideas on a continuous basis. The idea development process and the opportunity assessment plan provide mechanisms for ensuring that new ideas are forthcoming and evaluated in a systematic manner.

References

Hisrich, R. D., & Peters, M. P. (1991). *Marketing decisions for new and mature products* (2nd ed.). Upper Saddle River, NJ: Pearson.

Hisrich, R. D., Peters, M. P., & Shepherd, D. (2013). *Entrepreneurship* (9th ed.). New York: McGraw-Hill.

Suggested Readings

Fadel, S. (2010, Jan./Feb). Resources to encourage entrepreneurial creativity and innovation. *Online, 34,* 22–24, 26–30.

The author of this article is a business reference librarian at the University of Maine–Orono. The article is a helpful resource for entrepreneurs seeking information and resources from a variety of lesser-known publications and other outlets, including sample business plans as well as industry-specific information.

Fillis, I., & Rentschler, R. (2010, March). The role of creativity in entrepreneurship. *Journal of Enterprising Culture*, 18(1), 49–81.

Ian Fillis and Ruth Rentschler first explore the classical definition of entrepreneurship, which includes three major dimensions: (1) being innovative, (2) taking risks, and (3) being proactive. The authors investigate the link between creativity and existing entrepreneurs. They argue that entrepreneurs are best poised to act on the opportunity created by globalization and technological advances because of their predisposition for creativity. As a result, they are able to create competitive advantages for their organizations.

Girard, L. (2011, June 3). Five creativity exercises to find your passion. Entrepreneur. com, www.entrepreneur.com/article/219709

In this article, the author suggests five techniques for entrepreneurs in using creativity to find their passions. The author argues that finding one's passion is the fastest route to launching a successful business. The steps for exploring creativity are revisiting childhood passions, making a *creativity board* of images, making a list of people you want to emulate, doing what you love even before the business plan, and taking a break from *business thinking.*

Glinskiene, R., & Petuskiene, E. (2011, February). Entrepreneurship as the basic element for the successful employment of benchmarking and business innovations. *Engineering Economics, 22*(1), 69–77.

The authors analyze the importance of entrepreneurship for the innovation creation. According to their studies, entrepreneurship and innovation are interdependent. Entrepreneurial businesses are heavily dependent upon innovative products, ideas, and services in creating business opportunities. Innovation on the other hand is triggered by entrepreneurial motives. The main objective of this article is to present the strong link between entrepreneurship and business innovations as well as the use of benchmarks to judge the successes of entrepreneurs in promoting and deliver on innovating ideas.

Tucker, M., Dunlap, D., & Friar, F. (2012, May). Instilling the entrepreneurial spirit in your R&D team: What large firms can learn from successful start-ups. *IEEE Transactions on Engineering Management* [serial online], 59(2), 323–337.

The authors studied the innovation process of successful start-ups over a period of 9 years and have pinpointed what makes these companies more agile and innovative than larger, more established firms. The authors argue that it is important for large firms to continue "thinking small." The authors also present some of the main best practices that start-ups have adopted such as "small omni functional teams" and constant exploration of market potential rather than quantitative analysis. The articles provide examples of how larger firms can incorporate the innovative approaches of their smaller counterparts can coexist within their existing corporate framework.

CHAPTER 8

The Global Business Plan

W hat is a global business plan? What is the purpose of writing one? Are there some common aspects of a global business plan that are universal regardless of the innovation? Who is the reader of this plan?

Scenario: Ryanair

Ryanair was founded in 1985 by Christopher Ryan, Liam Lonergan (owner of Irish travel agent Club Travel), and Irish businessman Tony Ryan (after whom the company is named), founder of Guinness Peat Aviation. It started with a share capital of £1 and 25 employees. In July 1985, Ryanair launched its first daily flights on a 15-seat Bandeirante aircraft from Waterford, Ireland, to London's Gatwick Airport. Ryanair's first cabin crew recruits had to be less than 5 feet 2 inches tall to be able to work in the aircraft's small cabin. In 1986, Ryanair obtained permission from the regulatory authorities to challenge the high fare duopoly of British Airways and Aer Lingus on the Dublin-London route, and in May of that year, their first flights began from Dublin to London Luton Airport. The launch fare of a £99 return was less than half the price of the lowest return fare of £209 charged by British Airways and Aer Lingus. Both British Airways and Aer Lingus cut their high prices in response to Ryanair's. This was the start of the first fare war in Europe. During their first full year of operation, Ryanair had two routes in operation and carried 82,000 passengers.

In 1990, following 3 years of rapid growth in aircraft, routes, and intense price competition with Aer Lingus and British Airways, Ryanair accumulated £20m in losses and went through a major restructuring in 1991. Michael O'Leary was assigned the job of making the airline profitable.

He realized that the key to low fares was to implement quick turn-around times for aircraft with "no frills" and no business class, as well as operating a single model of aircraft. Copying the Southwest Airlines low fares model, Ryanair was relaunched under new management as Europe's first low fare airline. In 1992, Ryanair continued restructuring by reducing routes and fleet. Despite these reductions, passenger numbers grew by over 45%. In 1993, Ryanair's growth continued, and for the first time, they carried over 1 million passengers in 1 year. They overtook British Airways and Aer Lingus in 1995, becoming the largest passenger airline on the Dublin–London route. They also became the largest Irish airline on every route they operated to and from Dublin.

On May 29, 1997, Ryanair became a public company with a successful flotation on the Dublin and NASDAQ (New York) Stock Exchanges. The shares were more than 20 times oversubscribed, and the share price surged from a flotation price of €11 to close at €25.5 on their first day of trading. In January 2000, Ryanair launched their website and within 3 months became Europe's largest booking website with 50,000 bookings per week. To accommodate their growth in 2002, Ryanair announced the largest aircraft order by an Irish airline by increasing their aircraft order with Boeing from 45 to 125 firm aircraft with an option to buy 125 more. The value of this order exceeded €6 billion. Ryanair became number one in Europe in customer service, surpassing all other European airlines for punctuality, fewer cancellations, and least lost bags.

Ryanair's 2003 acquisition of Buzz, the Stansted-based airline, from KLM gave them immediate access to 11 new French regional airports and made them the largest airline operating at London Stansted Airport. Google named Ryanair the most popular airline on the web in 2003 and www.ryanair.com continues to be the most searched travel website in Europe. To celebrate their 20th birthday, they offered 100,000 seats at 99 pence, 100 times less than their 1985 fare! In 2006, Ryanair was the only airline to guarantee "no fuel surcharges ever" making them the world's first airline to carry more than 4 million international passengers in 1 month on 436 low fare routes across 24 countries over the summer of that year. There was a 20% growth in passenger numbers in 2007, resulting in a total of 51 million passengers. In December of 2008, they launched their first charity calendar, which featured their cabin crew, and raised €75,000 for the children's charity Angels Quest in Ireland. The calendar has become part of Ryanair's annual contribution to a designated charity each year. Passenger growth continued from 2008 to 2010, resulting in an increase in employment numbers and aircraft. Despite higher oil prices, the global recession, and volcanic ash disruptions in the spring of 2010, Ryanair's profits rose 26% to over €401 million.

Ryanair has come a long way since it started in 1985 with a 15-seat aircraft and a staff of 25. They now operate a fleet of 283 new Boeing 737-800 aircraft on more than 1,500 flights per day from 50 bases across 28 countries connecting 165 destinations. Ryanair currently has a team of more than 8,500 people and expects to carry 75 million passengers in 2012. To date, they have a 100% safety record: No aircraft has ever been involved in incidents resulting in death or serious injury.

Ryanair was the first independent airline in Ireland and the first budget airline in Europe. It is one of the oldest and most successful low-cost airlines in Europe. Its innovativeness and willingness to take risks has transformed the Irish airline market where other airlines like Avair failed to compete with the more powerful national carrier Aer Lingus. Ryanair is a clear example of an organization that has faced many different environments since its foundation, and like any other airline, it has been challenged by the current economic climate. However, what makes Ryanair distinctive is its commitment and perseverance to successfully manage and overcome these challenges and be the innovative organization it is today. At a time when airline companies worldwide are in difficulty, Ryanair continues to expand, announcing the opening of its 50th base and expansion into Paphos (the third largest city in Cyprus) in May 2012 with 14 routes that will initially deliver over 600,000 passengers annually and sustain over 600 jobs with over 80 weekly flights. Ryanair will invest over $140 million at Paphos Airport.

Ryanair clearly leads the way in how they manage innovation and entrepreneurship in diverse economic climates through their strategies and philosophy toward achieving their goals. This is best accomplished by Ryanair as well as all existing and start-up companies through developing a global business plan.

SOURCE: Adapted from www.ryanair.com

What Is a Global Business Plan?

A global business plan is a document prepared by an inventor or entrepreneur that describes all the aspects of making the innovation into a new venture. Just like the Ryanair innovation, each innovative idea needs to have a road map or game plan to move forward answering these basic questions: Where am I now? What do I want to become? And, how do I get there?

In establishing the direction of the innovation, the business plan takes into account such external factors as the economy, competition, trends, and changes in technology. It establishes short-term and long-term objectives and plans for the next 5 years.

Purpose of a Business Plan

A business plan is written for several purposes—the most frequent one being to obtain financing for the innovation at some stage in its development. The earlier in development the innovation is, the more difficult it is to obtain the financial resources needed. Once the product/service innovation has been fully developed and even better when it has some revenue funding is somewhat easier to obtain. Both of these cases cause the valuation of the innovation to increase, allowing less equity to be exchanged for the funding. Regardless of the development stage of the innovation, the amount of capital needed, or whether the type of the capital is in the form of debt, equity, or a grant, a business plan allows the provider of the money to be able to access the innovation and its potential success as a basis of a new venture or a license on the market.

While financing is the major purpose for the creation of a business plan, a business plan also indicates the resources needed in addition to financial ones. By laying out the existing resources of the scientists and others involved in the innovation, resource needs are identified. These may include such things as technology, scientific equipment, outsourcing entities, distribution channels, scientific and management skills and experience, and sources of supply. Not only should the needed resources be identified but approaches should be developed in the business plan for their obtainment.

The third reason for a business plan—establishing the direction for the future development and launch of the innovation—is important enough that all innovations should have a basic business plan. Not having a direction established can cost much more to develop the innovation to the extent that the innovation may never be developed and commercialized. Having the direction established also helps provide focus for the creative individuals developing the innovation. Creative people find many things interesting and can easily have their attention diverted. Venture capitalists, entrepreneurs, and successful inventors all agree that focus is one of the most important aspects for success.

A business plan also provides a way to evaluate the results of efforts on a regular basis. These periodic evaluations allow the development to stay on track and generate reports for stakeholders such as fund providers. The information also indicates the deviations occurring, allowing the deployment of "management by deviation" or successfully moving the innovation development forward by seeing what needs to be done to correct the problem and get back on the plan or, in some cases, change the plan itself.

The final purpose of a business plan is to provide a document for obtaining the needed resources, outsourcing partners, or another partner.

It is much easier for some company or individual to become involved with an innovation when the direction and end result are clearly defined.

Aspects of a Business Plan

Regardless of its purpose, a business plan has several aspects that are necessary for any innovation. As indicated in Table 8.1, a business plan typically has three sections. Section 1 introduces the plan, Section 2 is the main body of the plan, and Section 3 supplies support documents for or expands on various items mentioned in Section 2. Each section will be discussed in turn.

Table 8.1 Aspects of a Business Plan

Section 1:	Title Page
	Table of Contents
	Executive Summary

Section 2:

1.0 Description of Business	2.0 Description of Industry
• Description of the Venture • Product(s) and/or Service(s) • Type of Industry • Mission Statement • Business Model	• Future Outlook and Trends • Analysis of Competitors • Industry and Market Forecasts
3.0 Technology Plan	4.0 Marketing Plan
• Description of Technology • Technology Comparison • Commercialization Requirements	• Market Segment • Pricing • Distribution • Promotion • Product or Service • Sales for First 3 Years
5.0 Financial Plan	6.0 Production Plan
• Pro Forma Income Statement • Pro Forma Cash Flow Statements • Pro Forma Balance Sheet • Break-even Analysis • Sources and Applications of Funds Statement	• Manufacturing Process (amount subcontracted) • Physical Plant • Machinery and Equipment • Suppliers of Raw Materials • Outsourcing Aspects

7.0 Organizational Plan	8.0 Operational Plan
• Form of Ownership • Identification of Partners and/or Principal Shareholders • Authority of Principals • Management Team Background • Roles and Responsibilities of Members of Organization • Organizational Structure	• Description of Company's Operation • Flow of Orders and Goods 9.0 Summary

Section 3:

Appendices (exhibits)
   A – Résumés of Principals
   B – Market Statistics
   C – Market Research Data
   D – Competitive Brochures
   E – Competitive Price Lists
   F – Leases and Contracts
   G – Supplier Price Lists

Section 1

Section 1 has three major areas: (1) the title page, (2) table of contents, and (3) executive summary. The title page labels the innovation and all major participants involved and their title. Often a three- to four-sentence summary of the purpose of the business plan follows. The title page should conclude with the following: "This is confidential business plan _____." The line should be filled in with a low number between one and five and then a record kept of the person receiving that particular business plan and the date. This allows follow up to occur in 30-, 60-, and 90-day intervals if no response is received.

The table of contents allows the reader to quickly locate any particular information desired. All pages should be sequentially numbered as should each table, figure, or other document appearing in the appendices (exhibit) in Section 3.

The third part of Section 1 is the executive summary. This important two-page document summarizes the main aspects of the business plan determined by the reader, purpose, and stage of development of the innovation. For example, if the innovation is almost developed and the purpose of the business plan is to obtain financing for the reader to launch the innovation, then the executive summary would emphasize (1) the management team and entrepreneurs; (2) the nature of the innovation, its competitive position, and unique differences and the size and nature of the market; and (3) the revenues and profits expected over the next 5 years. Five years is the usual time frame as that is the input required by most investors and the software program typically used by private investor groups frequently called angel groups.

Section 2

The main body of the business plan appears in Section 2 and contains seven, eight, or nine parts depending mostly on the type of innovation. The parts that may or may not be represented are the technology plan and the production plan. While there are several different ways a business plan can be laid out, the one indicated in Table 8.1 has been well received when used for a variety of purposes by the author.

The first part of Section 2 is the description of the business. This part describes in as much detail as possible the type of business being created and all aspects of the innovation and the resulting product(s)/service(s). A discussion of the industry of the innovation and its general characteristics position the innovation appropriately. This discussion is followed by the mission statement of the venture. A mission statement describes the overall main purpose and direction of the venture. It indicates the values and what is important. The core of the mission statements of several companies such as 3M, American Express, Ford, IBM, Marriott, Nordstrom, Procter & Gamble (P&G), Walmart, and Walt Disney are indicated in Table 8.2. Many common core features occur in these mission statements, including product/service excellence, honesty and integrity, respect for the individual employee, great customer service, continually innovate, and a customer satisfaction focus.

The final part of the description of the business is the business model. The business model has become an increasingly important part of the business plan as it gives an entire picture of how the venture will operate together with all of its strategies and tactics. It describes the innovation and how it will be produced and marketed. When the business model created actually is new and can change the way business is done in an industry, it is particularly beneficial. For example, Pizza Hut changed the pizza industry business model by introducing delivery. Dell changed the business model of the personal computer industry by building computers to order.

The next area of Section 2 is the description of the industry. The country code of the product in the respective country needs to be identified so that

Table 8.2 Core of Mission Statements of Selected U.S. Companies

3M	• Innovation; "Thou shalt not kill a new product idea" • Absolute integrity • Respect for individual initiative and personal growth • Tolerance for honest mistakes • Product quality and reliability
American Express	• Heroic customer service • Worldwide reliability of services • Encouragement of individual initiative
Ford	• People as the source of our strength • Products as the "end result of our efforts" (we care about cars) • Profits as a necessary means and measure for our success • Basic honesty and integrity
General Electric	• Improving the quality of life through technology and innovation • Interdependent balance between responsibility to customers, employees, society, and shareholders (no clear hierarchy) • Individual responsibility and opportunity • Honesty and integrity
IBM	• Give full consideration to the individual employee • Spend a lot of time making customers happy • Go the last mile to do things right; seek superiority in all we undertake
Marriott	• Friendly service and excellent value (customers are guests); "make people away from home feel that they're among friends and really wanted" • People are number 1—treat them well, expect a lot, and the rest will follow • Work hard, yet keep it fun • Continual self-improvement • Overcoming adversity to build character
Nordstrom	• Service to the customer above all else • Hard work and productivity • Continuous improvement, never being satisfied • Excellence in reputation, being part of something special
Procter & Gamble	• Product excellence • Continuous self-improvement • Honesty and fairness • Respect and concern for the individual

Walmart	• "We exist to provide to our customers"—to make their lives better via lower prices and greater selection; all else is secondary • Swim upstream, buck conventional wisdom • Be in partnership with employees • Work with passion, commitment, and enthusiasm • Run lean • Pursue ever-higher goals
Walt Disney	• No cynicism allowed • Fanatical attention to consistency and detail • Continuous progress via creativity, dreams, and imagination • Fanatical control and preservation of Disney's "magic" image • "To bring happiness to millions" and to celebrate, nurture, and promulgate "wholesome American values"

industry statistics can be gathered. This country code is the North American Industry Classification System (NAICS) code in the United States and the Standard Industrial Classification (SIC) in Korea and a different SIC in China. Data on the industry over at least the past 3 years should be collected so that a trend is apparent. The growth rate of the industry should be cited. Also, all competitors of the innovation should be identified and at least the ones closest to the innovation should be thoroughly discussed so that the uniqueness of the innovation is shown. Each successful innovation needs to have at least three to five unique features called *unique selling propositions*.

The next area of the business plan is the technology plan (see Table 8.1). This section may or may not be in a business plan depending on the technology of the innovation. Where there is a patent granted or pending then it should be discussed in the technology plan. The technology needs to be described in detail, indicating how the technology features of the innovation are better than those presently on the market and can produce benefits for the user. All commercialization requirements should be described by providing an understanding that the innovation can be produced in a systematic sustainable way.

The technology plan is followed by the marketing plan. The marketing plan starts with a discussion of the market, its size, trends, and growth rate. In a business-to-business (B2B) market, this will involve finding the country system number for the market similar to the industry analysis. In a business-to-consumer (B2C) market, this involves demographic data on the market. The typical demographic variables used are age, income, and gender.

Following the discussion of the market are the four major elements of the marketing plan: (1) price, (2) distribution, (3) promotion, and (4) product or service. Parts of each of these are indicated in Table 8.3. A detailed marketing plan needs to be developed for the innovation so that sales and revenues occur. The packaging, where applicable, and use of social media can be extremely important. Of all the areas of the marketing plan, price is probably the most difficult one. Not only do the costs of the innovation need to be carefully determined but competitive prices and customers' view of price need to be examined as well. In many cases, the innovation is priced too low. The marketing plan ends in first-year sales, which logically flows into the next area of the business plan: the financial plan.

Table 8.3 The Marketing Plan

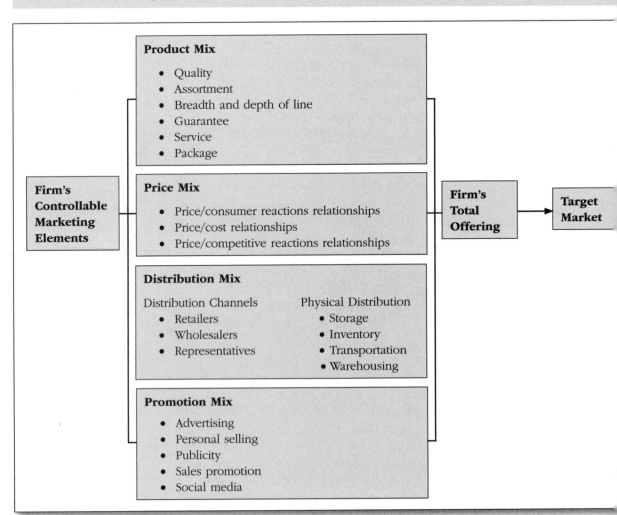

The financial plan—the fifth area of Section 2 of the business plan—has the 12 financial statements indicated in Table 8.4. The one different statement from the financial statements regularly seen in an operational business is the sources and uses of funds statements where the uses of the capital and the sources for this capital are indicated. Of course since the venture does not have actual numbers, all the income and cash flow statements as well as the balance sheets are pro forma or forecasted. In a start-up venture, the most important financial statements are the 5-year pro forma income statement summary and the 5-year pro forma cash flow statement summary.

Table 8.4 Financial Statements

- Sources and Uses of Funds Statement
- Pro forma Income Statement – 5 year summary
- Pro forma Income Statement – first year by month
- Pro forma Income Statement – second year by quarter
- Pro forma Income Statement – third year by quarter
- Pro forma Cash Flow Statement – 5 year summary
- Pro forma Cash Flow Statement – first year by month
- Pro forma Cash Flow Statement – second year by quarter
- Pro forma Cash Flow Statement – third year by quarter
- Pro forma Balance Sheet – Year 1
- Pro forma Balance Sheet – Year 2
- Pro forma Balance Sheet – Year 3

Following the financial plan is the production plan. This may or may not be present depending on the nature of the innovation. Many innovations are service-oriented in nature. The product plan can become an outsourcing or licensing plan if the intention is to either outsource or license the innovation to be produced by someone outside the venture.

The organization plan is the next area of Section 2 of the business plan. This focuses on the organizational form (type of venture) and the organizational structure. Besides proprietorships or partnerships, there are six general types of corporations available to be the organizational form of the venture: (1) LLC, (2) SC, (3) C corporation, (4) professional corporation, (5) nonprofit corporation, and (6) hybrid corporation. Care should be taken to understand the aspects of each type of organizational form in terms of legal liability, taxes, ownership numbers and location, and fringe benefit packages in selecting the best organizational form for the innovation.

The second part of the organization plan is the organizational structure. This usually takes the form of an organizational chart with the duties and responsibilities of each position delineated. Individuals already a part of the organization should be discussed by position showing their skill, education, and background.

The last two parts of Section 2 of the business plan—the operational plan and summary—are short ones. The operational plan presents a description of the operations of the venture, indicating the flow of production, orders, and revenue. A particularly important aspect of this part, when equity investment comes from outside sources, is the exit plan. Equity investors anticipate a return on their investment ideally within 5 to 7 years except for very high technology innovations such as biotechnology. There are three ways for this exit to occur. They can get their investment and return through retained earnings of the venture, sale of the venture to another company, or an initial public offering (becoming a publicly traded company). Most exits occur through the sale of all or part of the venture. Section 2 of the business plan concludes with a summary—a brief, overall summary of the entire plan.

Section 3 of the business plan contains appendices (exhibits) adding to or supporting information in Section 2 (see Table 8.1). Each business plan will contain a résumé of each principal person involved. Also, typical appendices are market statistics, market research data, competitive brochures, competitive price lists, leases and contracts, and supplier price lists.

Implementing the Business Plan

The business plan is designed to guide the development of the innovation into an operationalized new venture. In order for this to occur, controls need to be put in place to monitor the activities. Some of the usual controls include development control, quality control, inventory control, production control, sales control, cash flow control, and distribution control. It is particularly important to focus on the market entry strategy to avoid sales occurring much later than expected and costs exceeding expectations.

Even the most effective business plan actually becomes out of date as soon as it is implemented. A business plan needs to be revised as needed, reflecting the changes in the customers, economy, competition, industry, technology, and results of operation.

Even good business plans can result in failure to successfully commercialize an innovation. Typical causes include lack of market acceptance of the innovation, cost overruns, unrealistic objectives, lack of capital, and lack of management experience and expertise. In spite of this, an innovation has a better chance of success with a business plan than without one.

Summary

This chapter took an innovation through the process of creating a business plan. By examining the internal and external factors affecting the innovation and its successful commercialization, the business plan provides important guidance in decision making and venture creation. Given the high rate of failure of commercialization, every effort should be made to create a plan that can be executed in a timely, cost effective manner.

Suggested Readings

Henricks, M. (2008, December). Do you really need a business plan? *Entrepreneur.*

The article showcases the cofounder and co-owner of Roaring Lion Energy Drink, Sean Hackney, and his philosophy on writing a business plan. The entrepreneur considers the business plan the cornerstone of every new business and a live document that should be subject to frequent revisions.

Kwicien, J. (2011, March). Enhance your asset value with a business plan. *Employee Benefit Adviser*, 56.

The author considers the business plan as a definitive action plan that solidifies one's commitment to the business. Jack Kwicien also shares valuable tips to create a business plan that will indeed improve the asset value of the organization. He also highlights the importance of including the company's employees in the creation and evolution of the plan.

Kwicien, J. (2012, January). Put it in writing. *Employee Benefit Adviser*, 30.

In this article, Jack Kwicien presents the business plan as an opportunity for the business owner to analyze all the issues pertinent to managing the business and positioning it as a value add to customers. He highlights the importance of treating a business plan as a concrete road map and guide to running a business.

Prince, C. (2007, August). Here's the plan. *Entrepreneur.*

This article focuses on the importance of the business plan to the operation of business enterprises in the United States. The author notes that a good business plan can give an entrepreneur a concrete vision of the future trends and long-term objectives.

Sahlman, W. (1997, July). How to write a great business plan. *Harvard Business Review.*

William Sahlman suggests that a great business plan is one that focuses on four important factors: (1) the people, (2) the opportunity, (3) the context, and (4) the possibilities for both risk and reward. In addition to demonstrating an understanding of the context in which their venture will operate, entrepreneurs should make clear how they will respond when that context inevitably changes.

MAKING IT ALL HAPPEN: THE FUTURE OF INNOVATION AND ENTREPRENEURSHIP

CHAPTER 9

International Opportunities for Innovation and Entrepreneurship

What factors influence the level and direction of innovation and entrepreneurship in the domestic market? Do these influential factors change in the context of international businesses? How can both domestic and international businesses achieve growth through innovation and entrepreneurship? How can this growth be stimulated and sustained in the context of diverse, challenging, and fast-changing environments?

Scenario: Unilever

Innovation and vision led to the creation of a global leader that has changed the lives of customers and employees all over the world. That company is Unilever. Unilever was established in 1930. In the late 19th century, the businesses that became known as Unilever were among the most philanthropic of their time. They developed projects to create a positive social impact, enhancing hygiene and personal care for all members of society and improving nutrition by adding important vitamins to foods.

At Oss in Brabant, the Netherlands, in the late 19th century, two family businesses of butter merchants, Jurgens and Van den Bergh, had thriving export trades to the United Kingdom. In the early 1870s, product innovation began as they became interested in a new product known as margarine, which was an affordable substitute for butter. By 1898, Van den Bergh had a sales force of 750 and launched a new branded margarine know as Vitello. In 1885, William Lever who ran a successful wholesale family grocery business started producing a new type of household soap. By 1895, UK Lever Brothers had annual sales of approximately 40,000 tons of Sunlight soap and started their European, American, and British colonies expansion.

By the early 20th century, margarine and soap producing businesses started to move into the same market, which intensified competition. In 1910, the challenging economic conditions and the First World War made trading difficult; therefore, businesses formed trade associations to protect their shared interests. In 1917, in preparation for expansion into North America, Lever Brothers acquired Pears Soap, and Jurgens formed an alliance with Kellogg's. Jurgens and Van den Bergh both established factories in England with one in Purfleet, Essex, that still manufactures margarine today.

In 1927, Jurgens and Van den Bergh joined together to create Margarine Unie. On September 2, 1929, in one of the biggest mergers of its time, Lever Brothers and Margarine Unie signed an agreement to create Unilever. On January 1, 1930, Unilever was officially established. The 1930s was a challenging decade that started with a Great Depression and ended with the Second World War. This meant that Unilever had to urgently rationalize, cutting its 50 soap-manufacturing companies in the United Kingdom to focus on fewer brands. However, Unilever continued to expand through the development of new products in its existing markets and by acquiring companies to take it into emerging categories like frozen and convenience foods. This marks a true internationally entrepreneurial and innovative organization. During the 1940s, Unilever's international operations began to fragment, but they continued to expand in the food market. They acquired new businesses with a diverse product range, and they invested in research and development (R & D) for new materials and production techniques. By the end of the war, they regained control of their international network with the exception of eastern Europe and China.

During the 1950s, business boomed as a result of new technological development and the European Economic Community resulting in a consumer boom and improved standard of living. New markets opened in emerging economies worldwide with new types of food being developed in response to the requirement for more nutritious food. In the 1960s, Unilever expanded and diversified through innovation and acquisition. It started developing new products, entering new markets, and managing a highly ambitious acquisition program. During the 1970s, there were difficult economic conditions and high rates of inflation. Unilever continued to diversify in the 1970s, but it stopped supply chain expansion because third-party suppliers were bigger and more capable of taking over noncore tasks.

In the 1980s, Unilever was recognized as the world's 26th largest business. However, it decided to rationalize its businesses to concentrate on core products and brands, leading to large acquisitions and divestments. By 1989, there was evident growth of core businesses. This core focus continued in the 1990s as the business expanded into central and eastern Europe. They concentrated on even fewer product categories, resulting in the sale or withdrawal of two thirds of its brands. During the 1990s, Unilever set up a sustainable agriculture program due to growing environmental pressures and consumer concerns about the food chain.

The 21st century began at Unilever with the launch of Path to Growth, a 5-year strategic plan to transform the business, resulting in further acquisitions and the rationalization of manufacturing and production sites to develop centers of excellence. In 2004, it focused its plan on the needs of 21st-century consumers with its Vitality mission, which aimed "to meet every day needs for nutrition, hygiene and personal care with brands that help people look good, feel good and get more out of life." By the end of 2009, the economic downturn was worldwide. Unilever was founded in the 1930s, which was a time of the Great Depression and has successfully managed many diverse and challenging economic environments. Being flexible and capable of responding efficiently to fast-changing market conditions has contributed to their successful ability to emerge from recession(s) stronger than ever.

By the end of 2010, it was reported that Unilever products were sold in 180 countries, they employed 167,000, senior management team came from 22 different nationalities, 53% of business came from emerging markets, €938 million was spent on R & D worldwide, and they spent 13 years as Food Producers sector leader in the Dow Jones Sustainability Indexes. In 2011, Unilever built on its corporate responsibility credentials by entering the new decade with a new strategy: the Compass. The objective of the Compass was to double the size of the business and at the same time reduce their environmental impact. Despite the challenging economic climate, Unilever had a 6.55 growth in 2011 and growth in 60% of their categories. The biggest growth was reported in emerging markets and personal care with 11.5% and 8% respectively. According to Paul Polman, CEO of Unilever, appropriate measures are taken to keep competitive whatever environment the company is facing. The company is more agile and invests in innovations to strengthen brand and brand equity. Innovations are stepped up with a focus on being closer to the customer to better serve them in 2012. Polman believes that there are enormous opportunities in challenging environments, and Unilever builds this into their strategy to reap the benefits.

Unilever's history is over three centuries, and their success has been achieved in very diverse economic climates. The success and continuous growth come down to their R & D, which employs over 6,000 professionals in 20 different countries across the globe using breakthrough technology to get the best innovations into the market as fast as possible. Their ability to meet customers' needs, wants, and expectations in rapidly changing diverse markets and market conditions makes Unilever a true leader in innovation.

SOURCE: Adapted from www.unilever.com.

Introduction

In past decades, organizations had viewed the global sector as closed, where each country or market was considered to be separate from others. Organizations failed to recognize globalization and international competition due to more controlled economies with barriers to entry. Today's environment is very different, and international business opportunities are infinite. What were once controlled economies are now more market-oriented ones. Technological advancement and development now means that competitors are anyone that customers or target customers have access to and that can be nationally or internationally. On this premise, small and medium enterprises (SMEs) and large corporations need to think global. Markets have moved beyond the Unites States and Europe to the Middle East, which provides endless possibilities for innovative and entrepreneurial organizations wanting to expand and compete globally. As indicated with Unilever, organizations cannot stand still and survive in a fast-changing global economy.

Through globalization, SMEs and large corporations in all industries and sectors are now under pressure to internationalize. Because of globalization, location becomes a factor of limited importance in developing and maintaining international economic, political, and social–cultural relations. The national income gap between developing nations (e.g., Peoples Republic of China) and leading industrial nations (e.g., United States) are rapidly closing. The internal income gap between rich and poor is also shrinking in most Asian nations.

The globalization of entrepreneurship generates wealth and employment that benefits individuals and societies nationally and internationally.

Globalization provides innovative and entrepreneurial organizations with many new market opportunities. Combining domestic and international sales provides organizations with the opportunity for growth and development at a level that is not viable by staying in a domestic market. Particularly if competitors are expanding into the global market this would intensify competition further and make it more challenging to achieve competitive advantage. Therefore, it is fundamental that innovative and entrepreneurial organizations strongly consider the global market.

Organizations that embrace an innovative and entrepreneurial strategy, structure, systems, and culture increase the likelihood that they will identify and utilize their capabilities as a pathway to increasing performance. In the field of innovation and entrepreneurship, there is much debate about the measures of performance. Measures and metrics to drive innovation are complex largely due to the multidimensionality of innovation. Also, many organizations measure inputs and outputs and ignore the actual processes. Return on investment (ROI) and return on sales (ROS) are typical measures of financial performance. Organizations need to measure the process of innovation and entrepreneurship, as well as other measures of financial, non-financial and innovation performance.

This chapter examines the differences between international and domestic entrepreneurship and the role of key environmental factors in the establishment of an international versus domestic organization. The reasons why innovative and entrepreneurial organizations will continue to expand internationally, including global market conditions and growth in environmental and sustainable development, are also examined. In addition, this chapter discusses critical importance of selecting the right foreign market as well as understanding and ensuring appropriate ethical standards in international business. Following that, financial, non-financial, and innovation performance measures are discussed. Finally, the chapter concludes by presenting innovation performance indicators for each stage of the innovation process because measuring performance is not just important for the outcome of the innovation but also each stage of the innovation process to assess and evaluate that the actual innovation has potential to enhance performance.

International and Domestic Innovation and Entrepreneurship: Important Considerations

With more countries being multinational, the distinction between foreign and domestic markets is less pronounced because organizations have greater exposure to diverse cultures even within their own domestic market. Domestic and international innovative and entrepreneurial organizations are concerned with sales, profit, market share, differentiation, and competitive advantage and may deal with many foreign customers in their own domestic market. However, it is the diverse external environmental factors that affect their decisions and strategies. Therefore successful organizations are the ones that understand the diversity and act accordingly. International entrepreneurial organizations are more complex due to uncontrollable factors such as political–legal environment (e.g., tax, price, marketing, ownership, legal systems, national laws, and legislation), economic environment (e.g., currency rates, government regulation, inflation, interest rates, employment, income, productivity, and wealth), stage of economic development (e.g., infrastructures, electricity, communication system, banking system, educational system, legal system, business ethics, and social responsibility), sociocultural environment (e.g., understanding and being able to deal with diverse values, norms, behaviors, and ethical standards while maintaining appropriate standards of business practice), and technological environment (e.g., technological advancement and development varies among countries in the way that uniform products that meet industry standards in one country may be quite different in other countries making it difficult to achieve consistent quality standards. Therefore, new products must be created based on the conditions and infrastructure operating in that country).

It is the organization's ability to understand and adapt to those external factors not just in the domestic market but all international markets that they are engaging in business. On this premise, learning becomes even more critical for innovative and entrepreneurial organizations that are competing in foreign markets. This is because not only do these organizations need to learn and develop knowledge in the context of their innovations and markets and customers but they need to develop a comprehensive local knowledge and experience as they are dealing with a different culture, market, and environment. Without this knowledge, they are subjecting themselves to failure as knowledge is the primary basis of achieving and sustaining competitive advantage.

Development in International Innovation and Entrepreneurship

Increasingly, the need to operate internationally and the importance of recognizing the criticality of consumers for successful strategies influence the decisions and actions the organization takes to form and exploit competitive advantages. The globalization of innovation and entrepreneurship creates wealth and employment that benefits individuals and societies worldwide. Innovation and entrepreneurship will continue to develop in the future across borders, because of global market conditions, international collaboration, lack of confidence in economies, changes in the business environment, entrepreneurial mindset, and growth in environmental and sustainable development.

Global Market Conditions

There are fewer barriers to entry that make it easier to do business internationally. There is greater interdependence among economies. Technological advancement and development makes it easy to communicate and do business not just within the domestic market but internationally. Global market conditions drive political reform, cultural transparency, and social development; they also create value and wealth.

International Collaboration

This creates greater opportunities for more innovative and entrepreneurial activities. It extends beyond the organization's R & D department and creates opportunities for open innovation and user-driven innovation on a wider international scale. In turn, this collaboration may open opportunities for synergy, strategic alliances, and new ventures.

Lack of Confidence in Economies

The global economic crisis has resulted in the international credit crunch, rising energy costs, adverse exchange rate movements, property collapse, banking crisis, poor financial credit ratings, and a severe deterioration in the construction sector among others and high levels of unemployment. People have lost confidence in governments, large corporations, and financial institutions. This causes people to reinvent themselves as individuals, communities, countries, and societies. More innovations and entrepreneurial activities emerge as well as more entrepreneurs joining the field.

Changes in the Business Environment

This is required to accommodate the needs of rapidly changing market conditions and globalization. Innovation and entrepreneurship are being recognized as a key success factor (KSF) for sustained competitive advantage.

Failure to innovate will lead to organizational failure. Innovation and entre-preneurship are not choices but necessities in today's business environment.

Entrepreneurial Mind-Set

Entrepreneurs that have set up their own business or are part of a large corporation have the ability to recognize, understand, and take advantage of changing market opportunities and many have a global vision. They have an ability to think differently, use insights, see what others fail to recognize, visualize future innovations that have not been thought about, and identify opportunities that are new and innovative and are what customers want.

Growth in Environmental and Sustainable Development

In today's environment where there is a strong focus on sustainability, entrepreneurial organizations need to address this by adopting environ-mentally beneficial practices. A growing consciousness about the value of protecting the world we live in and sustaining energy will accelerate the demand for products and services that can accomplish this goal. Therefore, innovative and entrepreneurial organizations need to interact with the newfound world to move toward superior environmental sustainability.

Foreign Market Selection

When a national business is considering going into the international mar-ket, the most critical decision is selecting the correct market. Organizations need to ensure the right fit between the national and international market and make the appropriate adjustments. If the gap between the national and international market is too big and the product specification, market orientation (MO), and customer focus is so diverse, the national organiza-tion needs to find ways to either meet the needs and demands of the international market or find an alternative. While many highly successful organizations can drive the market, this is a risky approach for SMEs and large corporations that have not established their name and reputation in the market.

In selecting a foreign market, organizations need to evaluate the mar-ket in terms of institutions and policies, human capital, infrastructure, markets and capital, and technological sophistication. External environ-mental factors (political–legal, economic, sociocultural, and technological), competitive environmental factors, and previous experience of this specific culture need to be assessed. The organization needs to consider the overall market factors (e.g., market size, market demand for the product), market growth, and the actual growth rate for the specific product in the market. A comprehensive level of research must be undertaken to ensure that it is a viable market opportunity for the organization.

When sourcing available data, careful consideration must be given to the relevance, availability, accuracy, reliability, cost, and timeliness of the data as well as whom originally sourced the data. There are many official sources of foreign information at government agencies, website embassies, and intergovernmental unions. Organizations must ensure that the information is being accessed from the official websites and sources; otherwise, there is a question mark over the accuracy and integrity of the data. When analyzing and evaluating both existing sources of information and independent organization research, the organization needs to be very objective and carefully scrutinize and question each aspect of the results. Additionally, they should undertake additional scenarios to analyze what would happen if there were certain changes and measure the variation of results. This is important because of the level of turbulence and uncertainty in the current global environment combined with trying to achieve greater accuracy in the measures of results.

Based on all the research and analysis, the organization needs to select the most viable foreign market to conduct business. If the results and analysis are not favorable for any specific market, then the organization needs to recognize this rather than push for something that may not exist and could result in significant failure. Alternatively, if they have identified a favorable market then the next stage is to select an appropriate market entry strategy for the targeted market.

Ethics and International Business

Ethics can be defined as a set of key principles prescribing a code of behavior that explains what is right or wrong. Business ethics is focused on explaining what constitutes human welfare and the required conduct to enhance it. It is based on moral standards: These are impartial, take precedence over self-interest, and apply to everyone. Many organizations have a formal code of ethics and core business value statements derived from societal ethics, professional ethics, and individual ethics. Ethical codes refer to the standards and conduct that an organization practices in managing its internal environment and its dealings with the external environment. Such issues concern not only large national and multi-national organizations such as Apple, Boston Consulting Group, Cisco, Coca-Cola, Google, and Microsoft and SMEs such as 3M, Federal Express, Johnson & Johnson, Ireland Limited, but public sector organizations such as civil service and universities as well. The importance of codes of ethics is that it; clarifies the organizations' expectations of employees' behavior in various situations, and clarifies what ethical codes the organization expects employees to comply with in their decisions and actions. Every innovative and entrepreneurial organization should foster a culture grounded in ethics and core values. To generate more social good, organizations should promote and engage in more ethically, socially and environmentally responsible activities, as part of their corporate strategies.

Organizations must respect the cultural diversity that may exist between nations they engage with and aim to effectively manage all overseas business activities in ways that will enhance and add value to the development of local communities. They must assume responsibility for implementing ethical business practices, ethical codes and standards, and for taking appropriate course of action to generate awareness of it among all those involved. They must consider the contribution of organization's stakeholders, both internally and externally, and drive the development and implementation of systems that will help achieve ethical corporate behavior.

Ethical organizational cultures are those in which ethical principles and core values are emphasized. Doing the right thing managing an ethical business that is socially responsible is not always easy. However, organizations must act in an ethical and socially responsible manner. In light of the current economic climate now more than ever governments need to put greater emphasis on the development of high quality institutions that restore trust among members of society and enhance the quality of interactions among them. Society needs to eliminate unethical behaviors and attitudes through appropriate educational, legal, and economic efforts, which requires a long-term commitment.

Performance Measures of Innovation and Entrepreneurship

In the context of both definition and measurement, performance is a complex concept. From an organizational perspective, the consequences of innovation and entrepreneurship should lead to favorable outcomes such as improved current performance and opportunities for improved future performance. As innovative and entrepreneurial organizations pursue future national and international opportunities, management must continually assess the actual levels of innovation and entrepreneurial activity occurring within the organization. They must also measure the level of financial, non-financial and innovation performance emerging from the entrepreneurial opportunities being pursued. In the current dynamic and global environment, innovation and entrepreneurship involves a significant level of risk and uncertainty. Too many projects have a high chance of failure; do not fit in with the core knowledge, skills, and abilities of the organization and their members; and do not have adequate resources to complete in a timely manner. Therefore, innovation and entrepreneurship must be continuously assessed and evaluated by top management to ensure that appropriate levels of performance are being achieved.

Assessing and evaluating innovation and entrepreneurship requires measuring the processes and outcomes. Assessing and evaluating requires not only focusing on the actual outcome but each stage of the process that leads to the outcome. Therefore, corrective action can be undertaken throughout the process when there is a gap between desired and actual performance measures. This reduces the risk of project failure and substantial losses. However, to do this effectively there must be clearly formulated goals and objectives that guide and motivate innovative and entrepreneurial activities. In this context, is gives greater clarity so that the management knows exactly what they are aiming to achieve and can measure assess and evaluate performance accordingly.

Performance outcomes are based on a sustainable competitive advantage, and research has suggested that the more innovative and entrepreneurial organizations are the higher relative performance than organizations that are less innovative and entrepreneurial. Innovation and entrepreneurship are utilized to achieve increased profitability, and performance is usually measured by financial returns. In the current economic climate, organizations are facing a dynamic external environment with eroding tax bases, greater accountability and transparency, significant technological advancements, increased competition both nationally and internationally, and increasingly diverse stakeholders and customers to serve. Innovation and entrepreneurship can be a fundamental component that results in generating alternative revenues, enhancing internal processes, and creating innovative solutions to meet and exceed economic and social requirements. Performance as a multidimensional construct should be measured in terms of financial, non-financial, and innovation performance as well as the measuring performance throughout each stage of the innovation process.

Financial Performance

The conceptual argument of entrepreneurship–performance relationship focuses mainly on financial aspects of performance. Innovation and entrepreneurship can be utilized to improve financial performance. This is reinforced by a multitude of studies suggesting a strong link between entrepreneurship and financial performance. ROI is a standard and accepted measuring tool that organizations have depended on for hundreds of years. The problem is that ROI-based assessments generally focus on short-term thinking and tend to eliminate the development of more long-term, breakthrough, and discontinuous ideas and projects. Other organizational financial measures include average annual ROS, average return on assets, average annual return on equity (e.g., Antoncic & Hisrich, 2001; Zahra & Covin, 1995), and growth in sales (e.g., Titus, Covin, & Slevin, 2011) over a 3-year period. Furthermore, previous measures of organizational growth include two different indicators, combining subjective and objective measures. The subjective measure of growth considers the perceptions of the organization's CEO in relation what the organization's rate of growth has been during the past 3 years compared to other organizations in the sector. The objective measure of growth uses information from the organizations' annual accounts. This calculates the percentage of growth in sales for each organization over the 3-year time frame. Performance is also assessed relative to competitors in terms of items such as sales growth, ROS, growth in market share, and return on total assets (e.g., Wang, 2008). Table 9.1 includes a proven measurement instrument for assessing financial performance within an organization (e.g., Antoncic & Hisrich, 2001).

Non-Financial Performance

In addition to financial measures, there are several potential non-financial outcomes to evaluate the impact of innovation and entrepreneurship on organizational performance. Some of the most significant innovations and entrepreneurial activities do not generate measurable financial performance in the short term, but they define the organization and provide meaning to its diverse activities, thus enhancing performance in the long term.

Non-financial performance measures have a closer link to long-term organizational strategies. Non-financial performance benefits from innovation and entrepreneurship can in time produce financial results. Scholars have recognized the importance for researchers to consider not only

Table 9.1 Financial Performance Measures

Growth of your company: average annual growth in number of employees in the last three years:

☐ under 0% ☐ 0-4% ☐ 5-9% ☐ 10-19% ☐ 20-35% ☐ more than 35%

Average annual growth in sales in the last three years:

☐ under 5% ☐ 5-9% ☐ 10-19% ☐ 20-34% ☐ 35-50% ☐ more than 50%

Growth in market share in the last three years:

☐ decreasing ☐ holding its own ☐ increasing slightly
☐ increasing moderately ☐ increasing significantly ☐ increasing rapidly

Profitability of your company: average annual return on sales in the last three years:

☐ under 0% ☐ 0-4% ☐ 5-9% ☐ 10-19% ☐ 20-35% ☐ more than 35%

Average annual return on assets in the last three years:

☐ under 0% ☐ 0-4% ☐ 5-9% ☐ 10-19% ☐ 20-35% ☐ more than 35%

Average annual return on equity in the last three years:

☐ under 0% ☐ 0-4% ☐ 5-9% ☐ 10-19% ☐ 20-35% ☐ more than 35%

Profitability of your company in the last three years in comparison to all competitors that you are aware of:

☐ somewhat lower than competitors ☐ about the same as competitors
☐ moderately higher than competitors ☐ significantly higher than competitors
☐ a great deal higher than competitors

Profitability in the last three years in comparison to competitors that are at about same age and stage of development:

☐ somewhat lower than competitors ☐ about the same as competitors
☐ moderately higher than competitors ☐ significantly higher than competitors
☐ a great deal higher than competitors

SOURCE: Antoncic, B. & Hisrich, R.D. (2001). Intrapreneurship: Construct refinement and cross-cultural validation. *Journal of Business Venturing,* 16, 495–527.

multiple measures of profit but also non-financial measures. Important non-financial performance measures include commitment and satisfaction of organizational members', employee retention, process innovation, readiness for change, the gathering and utilization of knowledge, value creation for a diverse group of stakeholders, strategic repositioning, and competitive capability. Expectations of future outcomes are important for management and entrepreneurial decision making, particularly given the level of uncertainty of long-term outcomes that have been further heightened due to the financial crisis and economic downturn. Measures such as employee retention and satisfaction are important because when an organization loses a key employee, it is costly and has an inhibiting effect on innovation and entrepreneurship, a reduction in service, a negative effect on customer satisfaction, and serious consequences to the organizational profitability.

It is more favorable for organizations to use a broader set of performance measures as a way to improve the accuracy of the measures. This is particularly important for research on innovation and entrepreneurial activity at lower organizational levels. Multiple measures of financial and non-financial measures should be used. The combination should potentially add significant value for organizations in evaluating and assessing their innovative and entrepreneurial activity.

Innovation Performance

Innovation performance can be defined as the level of success achieved by an organization in accomplishing its goals and objectives in breakthrough, technological, or incremental innovation. Innovation is the major challenge faced by many organizations, and as a result, entrepreneurial activity is employed as the way to enhance performance and achieve innovative success. Entrepreneurial strategies result in innovations that renew and rejuvenate organizations, their markets, and their industries. The objective of innovation is to create value and generate wealth. Value can take diverse forms, such as the development of new products and services, incremental improvements to existing products, or reduced expenditure.

Innovation and entrepreneurial activity is now a necessity to give an organization every opportunity to survive and develop in a fast-changing, highly competitive market. The process of innovation is to develop and refine ideas into a viable form and implement them with the objective of achieving profitable sales or increase efficiencies in the day-to-day operational activities. Table 9.2 includes performance indicators at each stage of the innovation process and the commitment required by the organization throughout this process in order to enhance performance.

Table 9.2 Innovation Process Performance Indicators

Steps in the Innovation Process	Performance Indicators	Organizational Commitment Throughout
Idea generation/ opportunity recognition	• Number of ideas generated • Potential opportunity of ideas	• Innovation is a core part of organizational strategy • Top management support
Analysis of the relevant areas and facts	• Number of customer groups examined • Applications of research results in new products, services, and processes • Breadth of participation throughout the organization in the research process (broader is generally better) • Breath of participation outside the organization in terms of open innovation and user driven innovation • Time invested in research • Money invested in research	• Individual and team participation • Project management
Develop insights based on the analysis	• Number of ideas developed • Number of ideas contributed by our staff • Number of ideas introduced • Percent of ideas from external sources • Number of people inside and outside the organization who are participating in the process • Number of ideas collected in the 'idea gathering' system • Number of collected ideas that were developed further • Number of collected ideas that were implemented	• Research & development • Open innovation • Customer integration
Seek connections or bridging	• Percent of investment in non-core innovation projects • Total funds invested in non-core innovation projects • Top management time invested in growth innovation	• Learning • Knowledge building/sharing
Seeking creative leaps		

(Continued)

(Continued)

Steps in the Innovation Process	Performance Indicators	Organizational Commitment Throughout
Developing concepts	• Prototyping speed • Number of prototypes per new product	
Evaluating alternatives	• Number of patents applied for • Number of patents granted • Percent of ideas that are funded for development • Percent of ideas that are eliminated	
Selecting and planning for implementation	• Return on marketing investment • Number of new customers added • Growth rate of customer base	
Implementation	• Did the total innovation investment, managed through portfolios, yield appropriate results in terms of sales growth, profit growth, and overall ROI? • Gross sales revenue • Gross sales margin • Expected results compared with actual results • Percent of projects terminated at each stage • Successful results of each innovation • Cost savings achieved in the organization due to innovation efforts • Number of new customers • Percent of sales from new products/services? • Number of new products/services launched • Percentage of revenue in existing categories from new products/services • Percentage of revenue in new categories from new products/services • Percentage of profits from new products/services • Percentage of new customers from new products/services • Duration to market from idea generation to implementation • Customer satisfaction with new products/services • Growth potential	

Table 9.3 includes a proven measurement instrument for assessing innovation performance within an organization (e.g., Goodale, Kuratko, Hornsby, & Covin, 2011).

Table 9.3 Innovation Performance Measures

Please indicate the degree of importance attached to your business unit's top managers to the following innovation performance criteria. The following scale applies to all items:

NOT AT ALL IMPORTANT	NEUTRAL	EXTREMELY IMPORTANT
1 2 3	4 5 6	7

Number of new products or services developed	1 2 3 4 5 6 7
Number of new products or services brought to market	1 2 3 4 5 6 7
Speed with which new products or services are developed	1 2 3 4 5 6 7
Speed with which new products or services are brought to market	1 2 3 4 5 6 7
Ability to respond quickly to market or technological developments	1 2 3 4 5 6 7
Ability to pre-empt competitors in responding to market or technological developments	1 2 3 4 5 6 7
Incorporation of technological innovations into product/service offerings	1 2 3 4 5 6 7
Incorporation of technological innovations into internal operations	1 2 3 4 5 6 7

SOURCE: Goodale, J.C., Kuratko, D.F., Hornsby, J.S., & Covin, J.G. (2011). Operations management and corporate entrepreneurship: The moderating effect of operations control on the antecedents of corporate entrepreneurial activity in relation to innovation performance. *Journal of Operations Management,* 29(1-2), 116–127.

Desirable outcomes are only likely to be realized when supported by an innovative and entrepreneurial strategy. In this context, an entrepreneurial organization requires a strategic vision that focuses on organizational conditions that facilitate and support innovation and entrepreneurship and increase its willingness to drive and motivate individual entrepreneurial behaviors. Organizational conditions that facilitate and support entrepreneurship highlight the organization's commitment to utilizing entrepreneurial behaviors to recognize and exploit opportunities. In turn, this should increase the degree of innovation and entrepreneurship and enhance performance.

Summary

Global business has become increasingly important to organizations of all sizes and sectors in today's highly competitive global economy. Organizations today must be capable of engaging in the world of international business. The successful organizations will be the ones that fully understand how international business differs from purely domestic business and are able to respond and compete accordingly. The importance of innovation in the global economy, the significance of entrepreneurial activity for economic growth, and the critical value of strategic management for survival and success heighten the importance of innovation and entrepreneurial activity for all organizations.

The distribution of innovation is not equally distributed globally, and the location of innovation is influenced by the local availability of critical knowledge, skills, and abilities; internal strategies and systems that facilitate innovation; international credibility; R & D; external sources of technical and market knowledge; and external environmental adaptability. Organizations cannot dismiss the national systems of innovation and the international value chains in which they are embedded. Organizational strategies are influenced by their own national systems of innovation and their position in international value chains. In the majority of industries and sectors, innovative and entrepreneurial organizations challenge existing approaches in their search to generate value in more innovative and entrepreneurial ways. Organizations change the way business is conducted in the way they recognize opportunities and successfully fill existing gaps and limitations.

To sustain competitiveness, organizations need to constantly renew themselves. This can be achieved by providing required resources or expertise, championing innovative ideas, or developing a culture of entrepreneurial activity embedded within the organization's existence. Whatever form this takes, it must be continuously assessed and evaluated to ensure that levels of innovation and entrepreneurial activity are being achieved within the organization and determine the resulting level of performance. In order to assess and evaluate the process and outcomes of their innovation and entrepreneurial activity, organizations must use multiple measures of performance.

Innovation and entrepreneurship do not just happen and are not one-off approaches but need to be the vision of top management who must assess the current system and ensure it is connected to the accomplishment of organizational goals and objectives and improve performance and growth. It requires congruence between the entrepreneurial vision of the organization's top management and the entrepreneurial actions of those throughout the organization, as supported through the existence of entrepreneurial organizational conditions. The requirement for innovation and entrepreneurship becomes more fundamental as during turbulent economic conditions. Organizations need to be more innovative and entrepreneurial in ways that can contribute toward survival and growth and enhance performance.

References

Antoncic, B., & Hisrich, R. D. (2001). Intrapreneurship: Construct refinement and cross-cultural validation. *Journal of Business Venturing, 16,* 495–527.

Goodale, J. C., Kuratko, D. F., Hornsby, J. S., & Covin, J. G. (2011). Operations management and corporate entrepreneurship: The moderating effect of operations control on the antecedents of corporate entrepreneurial activity in relation to innovation performance. *Journal of Operations Management, 29*(1–2), 116–127.

Titus, V. K., Covin, J. G., & Slevin, D. P. (2011). Aligning strategic processes in pursuit of firm growth. *Journal of Business Research, 64,* 446–453.

Wang, C. L. (2008). Entrepreneurial orientation, learning orientation, and firm performance. *Entrepreneurship Theory and Practice, 32*(4), 635–657.

Zahra, S. A., & Covin, J. G. (1995). Contextual influences on the corporate entrepreneurship performance relationship: A longitudinal analysis. *Journal of Business Venturing, 10*(1), 43–58.

Suggested Readings

Brenkert, G. G. (2009). Innovation, rule breaking and the ethics of entrepreneurship. *Journal of Business Venturing, 24*(5), 448–464.

The author in this article examines a feature of the ethics of entrepreneurship that is rarely discussed: rule breaking. Specifically, this article defends a virtue-based account of the ethics of entrepreneurship in which certain instances of rule breaking, even if morally wrong, are nevertheless ethically acceptable and part of the creative destruction that entrepreneurs bring not only to the economy but also to morality.

Goodale, J. C., Kuratko, D. F., Hornsby, J. S., & Covin, J. G. (2011). Operations management and corporate entrepreneurship: The moderating effect of operations control on the antecedents of corporate entrepreneurial activity in relation to innovation performance. *Journal of Operations Management, 29*(1–2), 116–127.

In this article, the authors investigate the impact of well-recognized antecedents of corporate entrepreneurship on innovation performance. Specifically, the authors examine the moderating effects of operational control variables—risk control and process control formality—on the relationship between the antecedents of corporate entrepreneurship and innovation performance.

Kiss, A. N., Danis, W. M., & Cavusgil, S. T. (2012). International entrepreneurship research in emerging economies: A critical review and research agenda. *Journal of Business Venturing, 27*(2), 266–290.

In this article, the authors examine international entrepreneurship in emerging economies (IEEE) research. In doing so, they articulate its importance, timeliness, and relevance in consideration of the growing influence of emerging markets in the global economy.

Phillips McDougall, P., & Oviatt, B. M. (2000). International entrepreneurship: The intersection of two research paths. *Academy of Management Journal, 43*(5), 902–908.

In this article, the authors evaluate a special research forum on international entrepreneurship. The special forum reflected the fusion between international business and entrepreneurship. Overall, the article suggests that the work of scholars with experience in multiple countries must be combined with the work of scholars with expertise in multiple disciplines.

Rosenbusch, N., Brinckmann, J., & Bausch, A. (2011). Is innovation always beneficial? A meta-analysis of the relationship between innovation and performance in SMEs. *Journal of Business Venturing, 26*(4), 441–457.

In this article, the authors undertake a meta-analysis to synthesize empirical findings to determine if and under which circumstances smaller, resource-scarce firms benefit from innovation. They found that innovation–performance relationship is context dependent. Additionally, the impact of innovation on firm performance is largely affected by factors such as the age of the firm, the type of innovation, and the cultural context.

Zahra, S. A., & Hayton, J. C. (2008). The effect of international venturing on firm performance: The moderating influence of absorptive capacity. *Journal of Business Venturing, 23*(2), 195–220.

In this study, the authors apply an organizational learning framework and propose that the expected effects of international venturing activities on financial performance depend on companies' absorptive capacity. Their findings from 217 global manufacturing companies illustrate that absorptive capacity moderates the relationship between international venturing and firms' profitability and revenue growth. Their results encourage executives to build internal R & D and innovative capabilities so they can successfully exploit the new knowledge acquired from foreign markets.

CHAPTER 10

The Future Impact of Innovation on Consumers, Business, and Government

W ith innovation and entrepreneurship being so important today, will this continue in the future? What changes will occur in the innovation process? Is the speed of innovation and change going to continue at today's rapid rate of change?

Scenario: Local Motors, Inc., and Industry City Distillery

With a constant exodus of large-scale manufacturing from the United States, who would have thought that it would return and in such a unique way? In the past years, there has been a growing consumer interest in locally made, craftsmanship, and, of course, sustainability. This has caused a significant increase in small-scale manufacturing in the United States. A small company can cost-effectively create more customized products in limited runs using their design thinking in all aspects of the production. Sometimes this even involves inventing the manufacturing equipment or, even better, getting the customers involved in the design and build of the product itself. Among the companies doing this are Local Motors (www .localmotors.com) and Industry City Distillery (ICD) (www.industrycity distillery.com).

Local Motors, a Tempe, Arizona, U.S.-based company, provides a consumer the opportunity to build their own car through co-creation. Founded in 2008, the company leads next generation, crowd-powered automotive design and build. John Rogers, CEO and cofounder, who prefers to be called Jay, is passionate about cars and is building a game-changing American car company. A consumer is actively involved in both the designing and building stage (from sketch to production to drive-away).

Using open-source principles and assuring each consumer that only 2,000 copies of every design will be made, Local Motors is able to solve local problems and deliver through distributed manufacturing innovative, co-created vehicles and components. The company's core values are community, local, open, sustainable, and quality.

Through a large community of car designers and engineers making cars through open collaboration with people at the company, new car ideas turn into a reality. While not all car ideas become reality, the co-creation method enables a consumer to participate in the design process of the car and share ideas with other enthusiastic co-creators. The final designed car is manufactured in micro factories that allow this customization to occur. Their core vehicle, Rally Fighter, has a $90,000+ price point. Local Motors has received the CERA, ML100, CeBIT, and Popular Science awards and is one of several co-creation platform companies that include eCars–Now! (ecars-now.wikidot.com), MyMachine (www.mymachine.be/en), Quirky (www.quirky.com), Co-Creation (www.cocreation.pt), Open IDEO (www.openideo.com), and Open Planet Ideas (www.openplanetideas.com).

ICD was the brainchild of five individuals in their 20s who wanted to not only create a better vodka but wanted the vodka in a distinctively designed bottle. The company, the first one from The City Foundry research and design group, uses a uniquely developed custom-built glass fermentation system in its distillery. This original machinery was built in-house for this small-scale customized manufacturing process. The bottles and labels are also unique reflecting purity and utility. The clean letter-press labels are not the usual flashy ones reflecting a party lifestyle but have nothing more than the batch number, such as No. 2 and No. 3, and bottle number. Batch No. 2 had a production run of about 2,000.

As John Steinbeck, a great American author, once said, "Ideas are like rabbits. You get a couple and learn how to handle them and pretty soon you have a dozen." Will this idea of customized small-scale manufacturing involving the creation of production machinery and to the extent possible consumer involvement in the design and build process continue to proliferate perhaps at even a faster rate? Only time will tell, but it does have several aspects that make its future appear bright—local, craftsmanship, consumer involvement, and sustainability.

The speed at which innovation and change occurs continues accelerating. In 2012, Hans Vestberg, CEO of Ericsson, the world's largest telecommunications network equipment provider, said, "Change will never be this slow again" ("Ericsson Outlines Vision," 2012). To illustrate this point, Mr. Vestberg noted that it took 100 years for 1 billion fixed phone lines to exist in the world. In contrast, it took only 25 years for 5 billion mobile subscriptions to exist. By 2015, it is projected that there will be 8 billion mobile subscriptions, more mobile subscriptions than people in the world. And it is not only first world countries that have access to the network. According to Mr. Vestberg, by 2016, 90% of the world will have mobile coverage, up from 85% in 2012. As the network has expanded worldwide, the number of devices connected to the network has grown as well. Within the next 2 years, it is projected that two thirds of all electronic devices will have some form of connectivity with more than 50 million devices connected to the network. In this interconnected and rapidly changing world, the future of innovation will have significant impacts on consumers, businesses, and governments.

Impacts on Consumers

For the consumer, innovation makes daily life easier and creates more competition in the marketplace, resulting in more options and lower prices. In recent years, the Internet and mobile electronic devices such as smartphones and tablets have transformed the way people interact with each other and businesses alike, creating interconnected, networked, and empowered consumers who will shape the future of innovation for years to come.

PowerTrekk (www.powertrekk.com) is a "2-in-1" product: a fuel cell and a portable battery pack that you can use "off the grid" to power electronic consumer equipment such as mobile phone, camera, mp3 player, or GPS device. Born out of the Swedish Institute of Technology, this personal hydrogen fuel cell enables instant charging of depleted batteries without ever "plugging in." The mixture of water with some man-made friction is bringing a rechargeable electric source to people otherwise completely without.

Interconnected Consumer

As network access has increased, the ability of people and electronic devices to connect to the Internet—and each other—has opened a new world of communication. Most consumers today are connected to the world via the Internet, and a rapidly increasing number are connected to the Internet continuously via mobile electronic devices such as smartphones and tablets. Mobile access to the Internet allows consumers to go virtually anywhere and cost effectively, conveniently having instant access to information from around the world (Füller, Mühlbacher, Matzler, & Jawecki, 2009). Mobile electronic devices allow users to do more with less as consumers can check email, news, weather, sports scores, and train schedules from anywhere at anytime. Through various applications, electronic devices such as vehicles, home security systems, and even bathroom scales are communicating data to each other and consumers over the Internet. One such example of this technology at work is small tracking devices that can be attached to items such as a dog's collar or suitcase and once activated, it allows the consumer to track the device anywhere it goes through their smartphone, tablet, laptop, or online account. These technologies are enhancing consumers' lives by providing beneficial information they can use wherever they may be located (Berg, 2009).

Having easy access to the large amounts of information now available on the Internet is incredibly powerful and is permanently changing the behaviors and expectations of today's consumers. Consumers now expect to have up-to-date information regardless if they are in their home, office, car, or the park. Additionally, they expect companies to create user-friendly applications that allow them to easily access this information for a minimal, if any, fee. Demonstrating the extent to which modern technology is changing everyday consumer behaviors, a University of Colorado study found that 77% of college students use their smartphone before getting out of bed each morning, and 72% use their smartphone immediately before going to bed at night (Dean, 2012).

Networked Consumer

Consumers, interconnected via the Internet and mobile devices, are able to communicate instantaneously with each other, increasing their ability to share ideas, opinions, and stories from around the world. With a single Google search, people are only a few clicks away from reading the opinions and insights of thought leaders on any topic, as well as the thoughts of their supporters and critics. And as people are more willing to freely share their knowledge, the future power of the networked consumer is boundless. This new level of connectedness is changing how people communicate and interact with each other and with companies. Social networking sites such as Facebook, Twitter, and LinkedIn build upon the interconnected world to help users establish, build, and maintain relationships with others easily regardless of their geographic location. Facebook has over 1.06 billion user accounts from around the world. Internet calling companies such as Skype allow people to talk for free whenever they are connected to the Internet, demolishing previous communications barriers. Online dating sites such as eHarmony have revolutionized dating norms across cultures. And connected electronic devices such as the Xbox have changed how children play, allowing them to play games instantaneously against the neighbor down the street and a child from Japan.

Empowered Consumer

With easy access to the Internet and numerous mediums available to share their thoughts and opinions, consumers today are empowered to take a stand for causes they believe in. This new source of empowerment has significant implications on both business and government. Consumers are using the Internet to promote social causes, share news stories, publish self-produced films and artistic works, communicate solutions to problems, promote political viewpoints, sell goods, and do a host of other things. When it comes to companies, consumers are no longer willing to wait for goods and services but instead are leading innovation trends by actively communicating and advocating for product and service innovations desired. Consumer technology and access to timely information is almost equal to that of corporations. This puts consumers on the cutting edge of technology breakthroughs and in a reversal of roles, putting many companies in the position of trying to catch up to consumers (Coby, 2011).

One powerful display of human empowerment was the significant role that social networking sites such as Twitter, Facebook, and YouTube had in people's ability to communicate issues, attract supporters, and coordinate protests during the Middle East's 2011 Arab Spring. If the Arab Spring proved one thing, it is that governments simply cannot control the power of an interconnected, networked, and empowered populace (Dunkel, 2012).

Belkin's WeMo (www.belkin.com/us/wemo) is leveraging the growing trend behind the "intelligent home" where all aspects of the habitat are controllable and programmable. It intelligently connects all aspects from devices and appliances to activity and behavior inside the home through a programmable device that intentionally and rapidly responds to consumer adoption and expectations. It lets users define conditions and any desired effects of those conditions using "if this then that" rules. Furthermore, Belkin is using crowdsourcing to recapture user experiences and continually feed the development cycle of new "recipes." Those that are most popular are then used to retool the offerings of the default product.

Impact on Business

To stay competitive in this fast-changing, competitive world, businesses need to determine how to engage and interact with the interconnected and networked consumer. Proactive companies and participative consumers will engage together through social networking and open-innovation forums to create the next generation of products. Additionally, companies will increasingly need to design products and market to consumers in emerging markets. To do this, it will be necessary to create an innovative corporate culture that attracts and retains talented employees who will continue to innovate.

Social Networks

Companies are attempting to engage consumers by maximizing their social network presence. Companies are well aware of the potential impact of social networking, both positive and negative, especially when news can go "viral" through social networking sites in a matter of minutes. The public perception of a company through social networks has a dramatic impact on sales, employee recruitment and retention, vendor contracts, and government relations. Perhaps most worrisome for companies is that most information available on social networking sites about companies and brands originate from consumers, not the companies themselves. In a study conducted by 360i, it was found that "77% of YouTube, Twitter, and Facebook listings that appeared for brand searches were controlled by a party other than the marketer" (Meyassed, Burgess, & Daniel, 2012). This indicates the impact consumers are having as companies no longer control all of the messages communicated to consumers. If a company provides an excellent product or service, the information on social networking sites will reflect this. However, if the product or service is less than expected, consumers will share their negative experience with other consumers on at least one social networking site, directly impacting the company's image and future sales.

A company's ability to leverage the information on social networking sites can create a competitive advantage in the market. Making sense of the tremendous amounts of data that is available is a challenge. In a recent interview, Paul Coby, chairman of SITA, the telecommunications provider for the airline industry, noted the importance of leveraging social network information in the airline industry: "Business intelligence, and how you interpret your data, is going to need to become a lot more sophisticated. If you can get this right, you will be able to drive effective customer personalization, the key to loyalty" (Coby, 2011). An effective use of social media by a company can turn potential customers and employees into fans and sales agents through consumer-to-consumer (C2C) recommendations, rapidly decreasing the time for company and/or new product information to be communicated. With the addition of location-based social networking, the ability to directly target and market consumers most likely to purchase their products has increased. Location-based social networking allows people to communicate their locations, find their friends, track their dog, or even track their luggage through the airport (Berg, 2009). Although this technology does raise concerns of potential privacy violations, the benefits to the consumer are proving to outweigh the negatives.

Open Innovation

Innovation within companies has historically been an internally driven process that was secretive in nature. Given the recent technological advances as well as the rise of the participative, proactive consumer (Meyassed et al., 2012), the historical research and development (R & D) process has given way to open innovation models, also known as co-creation. IBM released the results of a survey conducted with 1,500 global CEOs, which concluded that "the most successful organizations are those that co-create products and services with consumers and integrate customers into the core processes" (Meyassed et al., 2012). Companies are learning it is beneficial to leverage the skills and knowledge of the intelligent and capable people outside of their firm and that people are willing to volunteer their thoughts and opinions for free. As a result, companies are reaching far beyond their company boundaries to tap into the thoughts and desires of individuals from different backgrounds, disciplines, and geographic areas. These individuals are not typically involved in the innovation process and include consumers, critics, employees, inventors, researchers, and even—in some cases—competitors. The widespread accessibility of the Internet along with cloud-based applications is bringing people together in real-time, collaborative environments supporting borderless creativity and innovation.

Open innovation models require some risk in sharing internal knowledge, templates, processes, and resources, but those risks are offset by the benefits of tapping into the knowledge and opinions of external parties. These benefits include (1) increased innovation effectiveness with costs decreasing and success rates increasing, (2) increased communication effectiveness as the individuals testing the products are familiar with the company and products, (3) increased speed to market as co-creation produces quicker alignment and acceptance of the final product, and (4) an increased ability for the company's products to stay relevant in a rapidly changing competitive market (Meyassed et al., 2012). Another benefit of the co-creation process is that the same consumers who help develop products often become the biggest fans and advocates of the products. Through social networking outlets such as Facebook and Twitter, these individuals share their excitement and involvement regarding the new product and this firsthand consumer testimonial increases the likelihood of higher initial as well as future sales (Füller et al., 2009). As businesses consider the implementation of open innovation models, they should not simply consider the costs of bringing the group together or the immediate financial performance of the innovation but also the long-term impact of increased customer loyalty and retention and converting these into increased sales opportunities.

Co-creation projects can range in their complexity and degree of interaction. In the most basic scenario, consumers interact with companies via their company websites or social media outlets and provide product feedback and ideas, which may or may not filter into the company's R & D processes. Sometimes viewed as little more than an elaborate marketing scheme, these co-creation methods are one way to create brand loyalty. At the other end of the co-creation spectrum, some companies have implemented co-creation as a business model in which they have integrated customer feedback loops into the core development processes. Consumers are actively involved from idea conception through development and even into the deployment process. This high level of co-creation is not appropriate for every company though, and most companies' programs fall somewhere within the range between these two extremes (Meyassed et al., 2012). And it is important to point out that the open innovation model is not only applicable to product-based businesses but also applies to service-based organizations. Henry Chesbrough, who coined the phrase "open innovation," discussed in an interview how service companies such as Amazon, Intuit, and UPS have successfully implemented open innovation models, working directly with customers, suppliers, and third parties to transform and improve their service offerings and overall customer experiences (Chesbrough & Euchner, 2011). Netflix fully embraced the open innovation approach when they published their movie prediction algorithm and awarded prizes to the individuals who most improved the algorithm according to criteria set by the company (Chesbrough & Euchner, 2011). Bill Joy, the cofounder of Sun Microsystems said, "No matter who you are, most of the smartest people work for someone else" (England & McLean, 2011). Finding ways to tap into the nonemployee knowledge base results in a strategic advantage.

Implementing a successful co-creation program can be challenging and requires the support of top management, a long-term perspective, and dedicated resources. Crucial factors to establishing a co-creation program include determining who should participate in the program, establishing the appropriate motivators to keep participants actively engaged in the process, and creating virtual tools that efficiently capture input and facilitate interaction between participants and the internal development team (Füller et al., 2009). In selecting the appropriate consumers for the group, it is often best to find consumers with high levels of product involvement such as information seekers, innovators, or opinion leaders (Füller et al., 2009). To encourage participants to freely share information and opinions, trusting relationships between the company employees and those involved with the open innovation group need to be developed. These relationships won't develop simply as a result of the group being established but must be nurtured and managed over time. Additionally, it is crucial that consumers feel their input is valued and appropriately used by the company to improve the quality of the products. Without establishing the proper group and environment, the long-term success of the co-creation process may be questionable.

A final point to consider in open innovation is intellectual property rights. In an environment where open innovation is quickly becoming the norm for R & D teams, the ability for a company to protect their intellectual property is becoming more critical. Unfortunately, in an open innovation environment, lawyers often discover a minefield of potential issues that must be navigated in order to successfully protect the company. Open innovation models increase complexity because contributors can be a mix of employees and nonemployees as well as can work from anywhere around the world. This exposes the company to intellectual property rights from many countries and jurisdictions. As innovation models continue to evolve, intellectual property lawyers need to be included throughout the process. Yet, both companies and lawyers acknowledge that the ability of rigid intellectual property laws to protect companies is becoming less enforceable in the highly flexible, iterative, global environment.

Emerging Markets

Emerging markets are rapidly changing the global competitive landscape, and companies must tailor innovation plans to meet growing consumer demands and prevent being overcome by new competitors. Based on International Monetary Fund (IMF) predictions, the BRIC countries of Brazil, Russia, India, and China will soon contribute more than half of the world's economic growth, outpacing the total GDP of the G7 countries combined (see Table 10.1). Accompanying this unprecedented level of economic growth, the middle class in emerging markets is expanding exponentially. There are currently 2 billion middle-class consumers in the BRIC countries with a collective

spending power of US$7 trillion. In the next 10 years, this middle-class popu-
lation segment is expected to balloon, growing to over US$20 trillion in spend-
ing power, twice as big as the spending power of the U.S. ("Trend #4," 2010).

Table 10.1 BRIC Countries

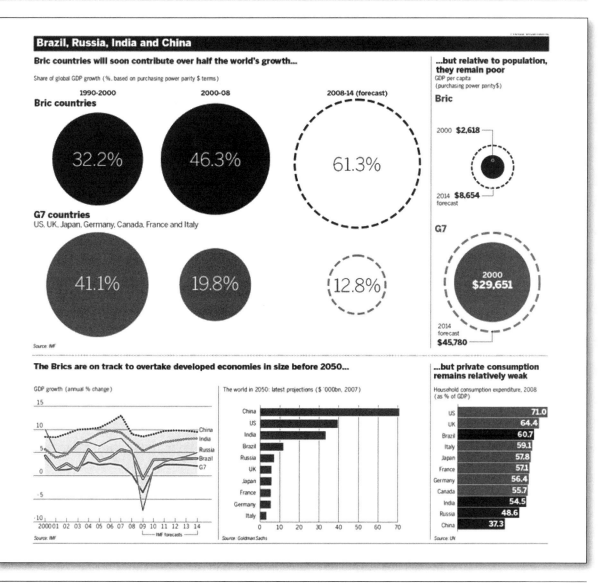

In traditional globalization methods, products were designed for sale to consumers in developed countries and then sent, with little if any modifications, to emerging markets and sold to the wealthy who could afford the imported, high-end products, thereby skimming only the top of the potential sales in the region. However, with the economic growth and rapidly expanding middle class, multinational companies are rethinking their approach in emerging markets and are adjusting their products and price points to appeal to this new consumer who is more interested in products that deliver an acceptable solution at a low price point. Additionally, as emerging market consumers become more affluent, they are quickly adopting modern technologies such as the Internet and mobile electronic devices. Following consumers in developed countries, consumers in emerging markets are connecting with each other to form social networks and are actively communicating. Responding to consumer feedback, SABMiller recently met consumer demands in Africa for lower priced beer by changing its production processes to use cheaper ingredients ("Trend #4," 2010).

The competitive landscape in both emerging and developed economies is changing quickly with local players becoming formidable competition to large multinational companies. Tencent (China) (www.tencent .com) has built a suite of communication apps and social networking plug-ins called WeChat. In less than 2 years, WeChat has become one of the most preferred means of communication among Chinese at home and abroad. Largely considered easier to use and of better quality than a telephone, it is a top 20 download in Apple's App Store and a powerful tool used to keep the expatriate community in touch with friends and family at home. WeChat is also engaging further development using an open source platform for its users to create and develop even more of what they want while keeping their first mover competitive advantage. Historically, multinational companies outsourced their production to companies in emerging markets, and over time, the local companies have become experts in producing goods and services. Combining their knowledge of production processes and intimate knowledge of the local needs, these companies have modified the existing products or created new products to meet the local demand, filling a void that was not being met by the multinational firms. This has led to the growth of mega companies in emerging economies that are now expanding outside their home countries to other emerging and developed economies. Huge multinational corporations are already competing with emerging market companies for business in other emerging markets. For example, telecommunications leader Ericsson now competes with China-based Huawei for telecommunications contracts in both Africa and Latin America. General Electric (GE) is facing a similar situation in their power generation division as they are facing growing competition from Chinese companies particularly in African markets. What many multinational companies like GE and Ericsson are facing are these competitors in their own backyards in the developed markets of the United States and Europe. Multinationals are increasingly aware that if they don't begin designing and producing goods to meet the local demands of emerging markets, then local emerging market companies could become a major disruptor in emerging markets as well as in the developed societies. This happens through reverse innovation, whereby breakthrough innovations in poorer countries migrate into rich countries. Perhaps one of the first major breakthrough innovations to do this will be the world's cheapest car, the Tata Nano. Originally designed for the Indian market, the Nano costs only US$2,500. Currently sold in India, Tata plans to export the Nano first to other emerging markets and then, after scaling up the Nano to meet Western tastes and regulations, to developed countries. Imagine the potentially disruptive impact the Nano could have on the auto industry in developed countries if a scaled-up model would cost only US$5,000 ("Innovator India," 2011).

In order to compete in emerging markets and protect themselves from reverse innovation competition, multinational companies will need a new, localized approach. Companies must establish a team within the country, give the team autonomy to develop products that meet the local needs of the people, and develop distribution and marketing approaches that make sense for the local infrastructure and culture. With more than a dozen reverse innovation teams now in China and India, GE is actively working to establish a reverse innovation approach, developing products from scratch to meet the needs of people and businesses in emerging markets. In addition to being highly marketable in emerging markets, these products are also designed for scaling up and sale in developed countries. One of GE's most successful reverse innovation products has been their compact ultrasound machine. Originally developed in China, the compact ultrasound sells for less than US$15,000, 15% of the cost of the high-end ultrasound machines GE sells in developed countries. Now a $278 million global product for GE, in 2009 the compact ultrasound sales were growing at 50% to 60% per year before the global recession (Immelt, Govindarajan, & Trimble, 2009). This product has not only been successful in China but also in the U.S. market for use in situations where mobility and timeliness are critical such as first responders. Similarly, health care providers across the United States need to provide lower-cost solutions, creating an entirely new market for products that get the job done, but perhaps with fewer features. Through their emerging market research, GE may be ahead of their competition in producing new products that meet this low-cost need.

Another key area of future innovation in emerging markets may be the creation of new industries around breakthrough innovations created out of necessity within the local market. India's energy situation provides an example of this as over 750 million people are still without access to electricity. Rather then building traditional power and grid stations as was done in the United States and Europe, India is more likely to take advantage of modern technology such as renewables, Nano power plants, smart grids, and micro grids to meet their needs ("Innovator India," 2011). Another example of local needs sparking breakthrough innovation comes from Fortis Hospitals in India that implemented the rigorous, disciplined U.S. health care standards but operate at a fraction of the cost by using a mass production concept whereby multiple routine surgeries are completed at the same time. This approach has allowed surgeons at Fortis to complete approximately 1,200 operations a year versus the 250 to 350 surgeries a year typical of U.S. surgeons, driving down the cost from US$100,000 for a kidney surgery in the United States to less than US$10,000 for the same procedure in India ("Weaving the World Together," 2011). This type of breakthrough innovation is setting the stage for a medical tourism boom as consumers from the developed world—seeking to avoid high medical costs in their home countries—travel to India for affordable medical care.

Workforce Recruitment and Retention

Maintaining an innovative corporate culture is a defining factor of a company's ability to maintain long-term success. The key to maintaining an innovative environment is attracting and retaining a talented workforce and creating a work environment that is conducive to innovation. In an interesting comparison between *Forbes'* 2012 "World's Most Innovative Companies" (2012) and *Fortune*'s "100 Best Companies to Work For 2012" (2012) rankings, nine companies made both lists (see Table 10.2).

Google, the top-ranked company to work for and the seventh most innovative company, has developed formalized, guiding principles, called the nine cultural cornerstones, to create their innovative corporate culture, attracting top performers and keeping them there (see Table 10.3). Additionally, without a dedicated focus on maintaining an environment of creativity, it is easy for a company to become too focused on short-term goals and lose the broader creative nature that made it great. Google works to maintain their culture by creating a healthy balance between their employees' day-to-day

Table 10.2 Forbes' 2012 100 Most Innovative Companies and Fortunes' 100 Best Companies to Work For Rankings

Forbes's Most Innovative Rankings	Fortune's Best To Work for Ranking	Company	Job growth	U.S. employees
1	27	Salesforce.com	39%	3,802
7	1	Google	33%	18,500
19	73	Starbucks	3%	109,477
31	63	General Mills	1%	16,939
34	6	NetApp	30%	6,887
61	23	Qualcomm	6%	13,353
84	19	Intuit	9%	7,102
86	76	Microsoft	.4%	53,410
95	80	Stryker	24%	10,368

SOURCE: Adapted from *Forbes, July 27, 2011 and Fortune,* February 6, 2012.

responsibilities and creativity through what is called the 70-20-10 rule whereby the company spends 70% of its engineering resources on core products, 20% on emerging areas, and 10% on wild and crazy ideas such as Google Earth (Gopalakrishnan, Kessler, & Scillitoe, 2010).

Table 10.3 Google's Nine Cultural Cornerstones

Creating an Innovative Culture – Google's Culture Cornerstones

1. Launch new products early and often, rather than trying to perfect the ideas

2. Believe in transparency in the workplace and open communication

3. Hire brilliant generalists rather than specialists

4. Allow employees to pursue their dreams

(Continued)

Table 10.3 (Continued)

5. Believe that data beats opinion

6. Keep employee generated ideas streamlined toward the company goals

7. Focus on creating products that are innovative and useful, not just something the company can sell

8. Don't kill ideas, but morph them into something useful

9. Believe that good ideas can come from inside as well as outside the company

SOURCE: Adapted from Gopalakrishnan S., Kessler E., & Scillitoe J. Navigating the innovation landscape: Past research, present practice, and future trends. *Organization Management Journal* [serial online]. 7(4): 262–277.

To keep the best and brightest minds, companies need a global perspective, attracting people from around the world. According to a 2011 *Economist* article, "The world has some 215 million first-generation migrants, 40% more than in 1990. If migrants were a nation, they would be the world's fifth-largest" ("Weaving the World Together," 2011). Due to the ease of communication over the Internet and relatively inexpensive international flights, this type of mobility is becoming more available to a wide group of people. Immigrants are an excellent source of innovation and bring a new perspective to companies. The most innovative companies are actively recruiting these transient employees and courting them with lucrative compensation packages and perks.

According to one report, over a third of Microsoft's 180 programmers in its Beijing research lab have Ph.Ds. from U.S. universities. Indeed, China is aggressively recruiting such individuals by offering incentives such as tax benefits, world-class housing, and extensive stock options (Teresko, 2003).

Impact on Government

Through innovation, countries obtain economic growth, job creation, and prosperity. Innovation also benefits a country by increasing competition, reducing the ability of monopolies to form, increasing product options, and lowering costs. Because most innovation arises from small entrepreneurial ventures, fostering entrepreneurship is important. Additionally, when larger, established companies know that energetic, entrepreneurial firms can easily enter the marketplace, larger firms are more likely to continue investing in R & D to stay in front of the competition. It is in the best interest of government to develop policies that create an environment conducive to innovation and entrepreneurial activities. Governments ensure the long-run innovativeness of their country through taxation, regulation, legal, immigration, and patent policies that are transparent and supportive to small and medium enterprises (SMEs). In addition to policy decisions, a cultural foundation that supports creativity, imagination, and risk-taking needs to exist for innovation to occur.

Employment Factor, Small Business Creation, and Job Creation

Job creation is critical to every country.

Of the 7 billion people on earth in 2012, 5 billion are over the age of 15. Of those 5 billion, 3 billion say they want a full-time, formal job. The problem is there are only about 1.2 billion of those jobs in the world today…a potentially devastating shortfall of nearly 1.8 billion jobs ("Trend #1," 2012).

Based on numerous research projects over the past 20 years, it has been well documented that small, start-up businesses create the majority of jobs and economic growth (Henrekson, Johansson, & Stenkula, 2010). In the United States, the Small Business Administration (SBA) reported that between 1993 and 2008, businesses with fewer than 500 employees created approximately 64% of net jobs (Valadez, 2011) while "Firms with fewer than 50 workers employ roughly one-third of all Americans" (Davies, 2010). Innovation creates three types of jobs: (1) direct, (2) indirect, and (3) induced. Direct jobs are created to produce the innovative product or service. Indirect jobs are created around the new innovation to bring the product to market such as new jobs at supplier and distributor companies. Direct and indirect job creation is evidence of the economic growth or increased GDP being created by innovation. As more jobs are added, more money will enter the economy and overall consumer purchasing power will increase. This will have a trickle down effect as consumers spend their increased disposable income in various sectors across the economy. To meet the growing demand in these sectors, induced jobs will be created, further increasing the country's GDP and economic prosperity (Alberro, 2011).

Based on the knowledge that small businesses create jobs and economic growth, countries should invest in development agencies that promote and support small business development and improve the likelihood of their success. In the United States, the SBA was established specifically to help develop and grow small businesses, and today the SBA is a strong business partner to many small businesses, providing lending, advisory, consulting, and training services.

Taxes and Regulations

A key motivator for inventors, entrepreneurs, and companies to bring new products to market is the opportunity to obtain significant financial rewards from the success of their invention. When allowed to reap the economic and social rewards of their innovations, individuals and companies are more likely to devote the time, energy, and money required to bring new innovations to market. To allow successful individuals and firms to retain the wealth they create and foster an environment conducive to entrepreneurial activities, governments need to enact tax, regulatory, patent, and bankruptcy laws that support SMEs.

From a tax perspective, almost all tax policies impact small businesses, including the taxation of earned income, payroll, capital income, asset holdings, corporate profits, stock options, and sales/use/VAT taxes. Studies have shown that "high and/or distortive taxes and heavy labor market regulations impinge on the creation and functioning of…entrepreneurship" (Henrekson et al., 2010). By keeping taxes low, governments will encourage entrepreneurs to enter and stay operating in the market. High taxes will discourage entrepreneurs to enter the market and will encourage existing companies to consider relocating, discounting business, or entering into the black market economy where business transactions are not fully reported to the taxing authorities.

In addition to minimizing taxes on entrepreneurs and small businesses, government regulations need to be limited to promote entrepreneurship. Regulatory processes act as a barrier to entry and as a fixed operating cost. Maintaining compliance with burdensome regulations, such as accounting and auditing standards, is time-consuming and costly for SMEs with limited resources. Regulations need to be simple, streamlined, and well communicated to ensure small companies are not put at a significant disadvantage to their larger competitors. Big businesses are well aware of the impacts regulatory and bureaucratic processes have on smaller companies and will many times support such programs in order to erect systematic barriers to entry for potential competitors. Government leaders must take this into account when drafting policies to ensure a competitive marketplace is present.

Intellectual property laws are also an important legal issue for inventors and entrepreneurs. To encourage entrepreneurs to invest resources, they need to have confidence that they will have adequate time in a market to reap the economic benefits and offset the cost to create the product or service. By enacting and upholding intellectual property rights, governments protect inventors and entrepreneurs as well as large companies providing time to reap the rewards of their invention before the competition can enter into the market. Today the United States is the primary target for intellectual property violations because, although the country represents only about 4% of the world's population, it spends 25% of the world's R & D dollars ("Trend #2," 2012).

Creating an environment that cushions people from failure is important to encourage entrepreneurs to take risks. The risk of failure should be minimized by having in place solid bankruptcy laws. By encouraging risk-taking behaviors, governments are creating an environment in which entrepreneurship can flourish.

Government-Sponsored Research Programs

Understanding the strong correlation between job creation and innovation, the U.S. government actively stimulates innovation through research programs. Many modern innovations that consumers and companies rely upon were originally developed through government-sponsored research programs. For example, location-based technology that enables cell phone users to identify their location through GPS components on their phones was originally developed by the U.S. military to track "missile systems, aircraft and troops" (Berg, 2009). Bar codes, CAD-CAM, fiber optics, the Internet, and web browsers were also born from public–private research partnerships (Teresko, 2003). One promising area of future innovation arising from government-sponsored research programs is nanotechnology—the process of manipulating materials on the atomic and molecular level. This technology could bring about radical change in numerous industries especially manufacturing, defense, agriculture, transportation, and information technology. It is also believed that nanotechnology will spawn entirely new industries not in existence today (Gopalakrishnan et al., 2010). For up-to-date information on nanotechnology and the latest developments, see www.nano.gov.

Combining innovation and education, the U.S. government has frequently partnered with universities to establish innovation centers such as technology transfer offices, incubators, and science parks (Gopalakrishnan et al., 2010). They have also been influential in working with local governments to develop technology and innovation hubs. In 2010, the U.S. Department of Energy (DOE) established the Energy Innovation Hubs Initiative to advance "promising areas of energy science and engineering from the early stage of research to the point where the technology can be given to the private sector" (Foley, Freihaut, Hallacher, & Knapp, 2012). The first of these innovation hubs was established in Philadelphia, Pennsylvania, where the DOE partnered with local universities such as Penn State, Carnegie Mellon University, Virginia Tech, and the University of Pennsylvania to develop the research. Due to the concentration of researchers, innovators, and entrepreneurs in innovation hubs, it is no surprise that these areas are hot beds of entrepreneurial activity and also boast higher rates of successful start-up ventures. Venture capital and private equity firms have also identified these areas and are heavily networked there, increasing start-up access to funding. As indicated in Tables 10.4 and 10.5, there are numerous research and innovation hubs across the United States and the world.

Table 10.4 A Snapshot of U.S. Innovation Clusters

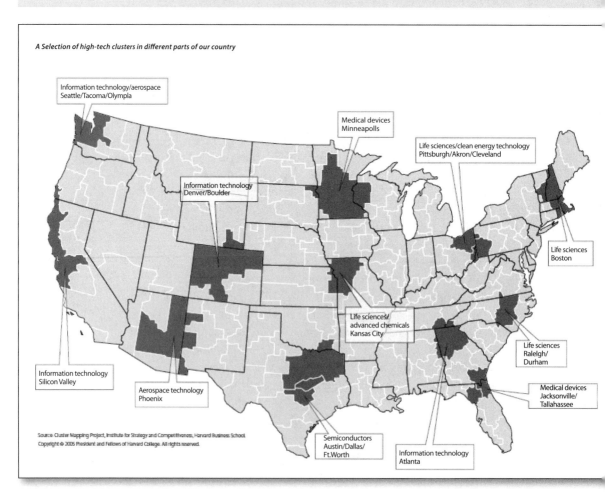

A Selection of high-tech clusters in different parts of our country

Information technology/aerospace
Seattle/Tacoma/Olympla

Medical devices
Minneapolls

Life sciences/clean energy technology
Pittsburgh/Akron/Cleveland

Information technology
Denver/Boulder

Life sciences
Boston

Life sciences/
advanced chemicals
Kansas City

Life sciences
Ralelgh/
Durham

Information technology
Silicon Valley

Aerospace technology
Phoenix

Medical devices
Jacksonville/
Tallahassee

Semiconductors
Austin/Dallas/
Ft.Worth

Information technology
Atlanta

Table 10.5 Global Innovation Clusters, Core Technologies, and Key Companies

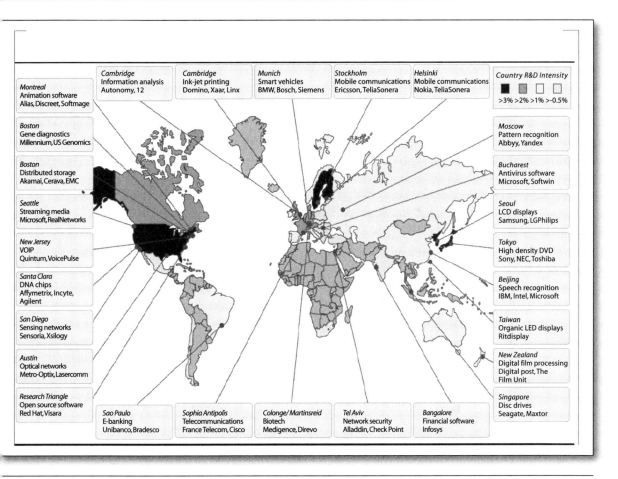

Montreal Animation software Alias, Discreet, Softmage	*Cambridge* Information analysis Autonomy, 12	*Cambridge* Ink-jet printing Domino, Xaar, Linx	*Munich* Smart vehicles BMW, Bosch, Siemens	*Stockholm* Mobile communications Ericsson, TeliaSonera	*Helsinki* Mobile communications Nokia, TeliaSonera

Country R&D Intensity ■ ▨ ▢ ▢ >3% >2% >1% >-0.5%

Boston Gene diagnostics Millennium, US Genomics

Boston Distributed storage Akamai, Cerava, EMC

Seattle Streaming media Microsoft, RealNetworks

New Jersey VOIP Quintum, VoicePulse

Santa Clara DNA chips Affymetrix, Incyte, Agilent

San Diego Sensing networks Sensoria, Xsilogy

Austin Optical networks Metro-Optix, Lasercomm

Research Triangle Open source software Red Hat, Visara

Sao Paulo E-banking Unibanco, Bradesco

Sophia Antipolis Telecommunications France Telecom, Cisco

Colonge/Martinsried Biotech Medigence, Direvo

Tel Aviv Network security Alladdin, Check Point

Bangalore Financial software Infosys

Moscow Pattern recognition Abbyy, Yandex

Bucharest Antivirus software Microsoft, Softwin

Seoul LCD displays Samsung, LGPhilips

Tokyo High density DVD Sony, NEC, Toshiba

Beijing Speech recognition IBM, Intel, Microsoft

Taiwan Organic LED displays Ritdisplay

New Zealand Digital film processing Digital post, The Film Unit

Singapore Disc drives Seagate, Maxtor

SOURCE: American innovation and manufacturing. *Trends Magazine* [serial online]. (2012, March). 107, 11-16. © AudioTech, Inc. Available from: Business Source Complete, Ipswich, MA.

Labor Force Education

Educating future innovators is critical to the long-term competitiveness of a country. Innovation is driven by human brainpower and creativity. Each country must assess the strengths and weaknesses of their education system and determine what areas to improve in the future. In a 2009 *Newsweek* article, researchers demonstrated that improvement areas differ by country. For example, Americans are focused on increasing math and computer skills while the Chinese are focused on improving creative approaches to problem solving (see Table 10.6).

Table 10.6 American and Chinese Parents Disagree about What Skills Their Children will need to Drive Innovation

	U.S.	China
Math and Computer Sciences	52%	9%
Creative Approaches to Problem Solving	18%	45%
Entrepreneurial and Business Skills	16%	23%
Knowledge of the World's Cultures	4%	18%

SOURCE: Figures adapted from McGinn, D. (2009, November), The decline of Western innovation: Why America is falling behind and how to fix it. *The Daily Beast*, 34-37.

Unfortunately, innovation and entrepreneurship cannot be entirely taught. Although courses can be taken at the undergraduate and graduate levels to increase an entrepreneur's knowledge of business and decrease the risk of failure, it will not teach how to be an entrepreneur. According to David Birch, the only way to learn about entrepreneurship is by starting a company or by serving as an apprentice for an entrepreneur for a period of 2 to 3 years. Birch estimates that most apprentices will burn out within the first 6 months and realize that entrepreneurship is not for them. Of the ones who remain, some will excel and develop their own niche in the market (Aronsson, 2004).

If a country has a lack of innovation and entrepreneurs, they may want to relax immigration laws and put incentives in place to attract talented individuals to their country. Immigrants are a great source of innovation because they often see the world differently than those around them who have not lived abroad. This different perspective not only leads to new inventions but it also leads to new businesses and job creation. According to the *Economist*, immigrants represented only an eighth of the U.S. population between 1995 and 2005 but founded 25% of all engineering and technology firms started in the United States during that time. It is important that countries develop policies that attract high potential, highly educated individuals. By attracting the best and brightest minds from around the world, a country's innovation future will be improved.

Culture of Creativity and Entrepreneurship

Underlying cultural attitudes toward creativity and entrepreneurship impact the innovation of a country. Although laws and regulations can be changed to be more innovation and entrepreneur friendly, if the culture of a country is conforming rather than creative, it will stifle innovation and entrepreneurship. Culture, unlike laws, is significantly more challenging to change and requires a dedicated, long-term focus.

Singapore is an example of a country where the culture was not conducive to innovation and entrepreneurship, which the government is actively working to change. Lee Kuan Yew, former prime minister of Singapore stated, "The greatest challenge to Singapore today is to get our people to move away from the old model. Just being clean, green, efficient, and cost-effective is not enough. You've also got to be innovative, creative, and entrepreneurial" (Hisrich & Al-Dabbagh, 2013). However, Singapore lacks a culture supportive of entrepreneurship. Based on their research, the Singaporean government found two of the primary detractors to entrepreneurship in Singapore were that "the educational system traditionally steered the most talented individuals towards careers in the public sector" and an "overarching culture of risk avoidance" (Hisrich & Al-Dabbagh, 2013). "Unlike the Western mentality that prizes original thought and individuality, the Singaporean ethos frowns upon selfish independence [and]…leaves little room for innovation,. . . having built the country on a doctrine of discipline and conformity" (Hisrich & Al-Dabbagh, 2013). The government knew it needed to change and that change would require significant time and focus. To kick-start change in the country, the government invested US$1 billion demonstrating their devotion to the project. Next, Singapore enacted laws to make it easier to start a business and loosened their already liberal immigration laws to encourage entrepreneurs from around the world to come to Singapore. The government's hope is that these entrepreneurs will become role models and that Singaporeans will learn from and imitate their entrepreneurial behaviors and business models. To further encourage risk-taking, the Singaporean government also launched an award program that celebrates entrepreneurs who failed in a previous venture but returned to the market and ultimately succeeded. Called the Phoenix Award, Singapore is hoping the award will reduce the cultural apprehension toward risk-taking (Hisrich & Al-Dabbagh, 2013).

Every country has unique perspectives on creativity and entrepreneurship that must be taken into account by policy makers to spark economic growth. Policy changes must resonate with citizens of the country as there is no magic combination that will work for everyone.

Innovation will be equally if not more important in the future than it is today for individuals, new and existing ventures, and state and federal governments. Understanding the fundamentals of this process is essential for the economic well-being of both businesses and countries.

Summary

Innovation is significant, and companies must innovate faster than ever before to keep pace and stay alive in today's competitive marketplace. Recent innovations of the Internet and mobile devices have given rise to a new consumer who is globally interconnected, networked across multiple communities, and empowered to voice their opinions, needs, and experiences. Today, the consumer is no longer based solely in developed economies. Emerging markets are emerging, requiring companies to produce new, lower-cost products in an increasingly competitive environment. Breakthrough innovations also promise to create new industries while disrupting and potentially destroying others. In addition to competing for sales, companies will also be competing for talented employees, as more of the workforce is willing to relocate for jobs based on salary and compensation packages. Without keeping a talented workforce, a company's ability to innovate is diminished.

Governments also work to maintain steady economic growth and job creation, both of which are created by innovative, entrepreneurial companies. To promote this entrepreneurial activity, governments need to enact laws that allow entrepreneurs to keep the financial rewards of success and minimize the financial costs of failure. By stimulating innovation through research programs and education initiatives, the government will bring about the next wave of business ventures and potentially entirely new industries.

This book has provided a framework for understanding innovation and entrepreneurship (see Figure 1.1). The origins of innovation and entrepreneurship were discussed in terms of the entrepreneurial/innovative economy, creativity and innovation, and the context of innovation and entrepreneurship. This was followed by a discussion of managing innovation and entrepreneurship in terms of building an innovative and entrepreneurial organization, developing innovation and entrepreneurship in individuals as well as teams, and design thinking. Operationalizing innovation and entrepreneurship was discussed in terms of new products and services and the usefulness of a business plan. The book has concluded with a discussion of international opportunities and the future of innovation.

The key is, of course, understanding the casual linkages between the parts of innovation as well as between innovation and entrepreneurship. When this understanding occurs, innovation value will be generated.

References

100 best companies to work for 2012. (2012). *Fortune.* Retrieved August 6, 2012, from http://money.cnn.com/magazines/fortune/best-companies/2012/full_list/

Alberro, J. (2011, May). Comment on innovation and job creation in a global economy: The case of Apple's iPod, by G. Linden, J. Dedrick, & K. L. Kraemer. *Journal of International Commerce & Economics, 4*(1), 89–95.

Aronsson, M. (2004, September). Education matters—but does entrepreneurship education? An Interview with David Birch. *Academy of Management Learning & Education, 3*(3), 289–292.

Berg, A. (2009, February). Social networking evolves. *Wireless Week, 14*(19), 12–14.

Chesbrough H., & Euchner J. (2011, March). Open services innovation: An interview with Henry Chesbrough. *Research Technology Management, 54*(2), 12–17.

Coby P. (2011, July). Changing the game. *Airline Business, 27*(7), 41.

Davies P. (2010, September). Sizing up job creation. *Region* (10453369), *24*(3), 18–25.

Dean, J. (2012, May 4). Smartphone user survey: A glimpse into the mobile lives of college students. *Digital News Test Kitchen.* University of Colorado Boulder. Retrieved from http://testkitchen.colorado.edu/projects/reports/smartphone/smartphone-survey/

Dunkel D. (2012, January). Social media, mobility and the future of security convergence. *Security: Solutions for Enterprise Security Leaders, 49*(1), 24–27.

England, P., & McLean, A. (2011, July). Don't forget the IP. *Managing Intellectual Property, 211,* 64.

Ericsson outlines vision for connected future. *Mobile World Live.* (2012, May 4). Keynote Address Video. Mobile World Live Web. Retrieved August 6, 2012, from www.mobileworldlive.com/videos/ericsson-outlines-vision-for-connected-future/22726

Foley, H., Freihaut, J., Hallacher, P., & Knapp C. (2011, November). The Greater Philadelphia Innovation Cluster for Energy-Efficient Buildings: A new model for public-private partnerships. *Research Technology Management, 54*(6), 42–48.

Füller, J., Mühlbacher, H., Matzler, K., & Jawecki, G. (2009, Winter). Consumer empowerment through Internet-based co-creation. *Journal Of Management Information Systems, 26*(3), 71–102.

Gopalakrishnan S., Kessler E., & Scillitoe J. (2010, Winter). Navigating the innovation landscape: Past research, present practice, and future trends. *Organization Management Journal, 7*(4), 262–277.

Henrekson M., Johansson, D., & Stenkula, M. (2010, September). Taxation, labor market policy and high-impact entrepreneurship. *Journal of Industry, Competition & Trade, 10*(3/4), 275–296.

Hisrich, R. D., & Al-Dabbagh, A. (2013). *Governpreneurship*. Northampton, MA: Edward Elgar.

Immelt J., Govindarajan V., & Trimble C. (2009, October). How GE is disrupting itself. *Harvard Business Review, 87*(10), 56–65.

Innovator India. (2011, January 9). *Business Today, 20*(1), 102–104.

McGinn, D. (2009, November). The decline of Western innovation: Why America is falling behind and how to fix it. *The Daily Beast,* 34–37.

Meyassed, D., Burgess, P., & Daniel, P. (2012, Winter). Co-creation is here: We can't ignore it. *Market Leader, Q1,* 36–39.

Teresko, J. (2003, August), Fearing R & D's flight. *Industry Week/IW, 252*(8), 20.

Trend # 1: The ultimate 21st century challenge: Good jobs. (2012, April). *Trends Magazine,108,* 4–9.

Trend # 2: American innovation and manufacturing. (2012, March.). *Trends Magazine, 107,* 11–16.

Trend # 4: Innovation and change become the hallmarks of global success. (2010, September). *Trends Magazine, 89,* 23–29.

Valadez R. (2011, December). The value proposition of small businesses: Economic engines for job creation. *Journal Of Management & Marketing Research, 9,* 1–11.

Weaving the world together. (2011, November 19). *Economist, 400*(8760), 72–74.

The world's most innovative companies. (2012, August. 6). *Forbes.* Retrieved from www.forbes.com/special-features/innovative-companies-list.html

Suggested Readings

Holman, R., & Jaruzelski, B. (2011, March 1). Casting a wide net: Building the capabilities for open innovation. *Ivey Business Journal.*

This article states that many companies are not able to fully utilize open innovation until the business is able to establish a culture open to externally sourced ideas and establish a program within the organization to capture and commercialize the ideas by examining the organization, culture, processes and tools, and incentives. The article concludes with an interview of 3M's chief technology officer examining 3M's success with open innovation through creating a community of collaboration.

Kashyap, P. (2012, September 5). Innovation in emerging markets. *Pitch.* Retrieved March 17, 2013, from http://pitchonnet.com/blog/2012/09/05/innovation-in-emerging-markets/

This article examines innovation in the emerging market of India. It examines reverse innovation using an innovation framework: product, process, and people. It also attributes the abundance of

innovation due to the lack of infrastructure and excellent social infrastructure and the need to continue developing a culture of innovation
at early age schooling.

Lerner, J. (2012). *The architecture of innovation: The economics of creative
organizations*. Boston, MA: Harvard Business School Publishing.

This book explores a formulaic approach to innovation creation
using incentivization and organizational economics. An exploration
of how innovation works and how it can be structured and managed is presented citing examples across various industries of
innovation-rich corporations and provides a framework for your
own organization.

Liyakasa, K. (2012, May 1). Game on! Games aren't just for kids anymore.
Companies are adopting gamification strategies to motivate customer and
employee behaviors. *CRM Magazine, 6*(5), 28–32.

This article examines the new trend of gamification, the use of
game mechanisms to encourage certain behaviors, and its application
by businesses to consumers and employees. Specifically, the article
gives an example on how an innovation management solutions company, Spigit, applied gamification to encourage innovation.

Miller, P., & Wedell-Wedellsborg, T. (2013). *Innovation as usual: How to help your
people bring great ideas to life*. Boston, MA: Harvard Business School
Publishing.

This is a discussion on how to create a state of "innovation as
usual" in the workplace by creating a self-generating ecosystem of
creative problem solving. This book highlights six actionable "key-
stone behaviors" as the formula for successful innovation: (1) focus,
(2) connect, (3) tweak, (4) select, (5) stealthstorm, and (6) persist. It
provides practical advice and ideas for those looking to innovate or
create an environment of sustainable innovation.

McQuivey, J., & Bernoff, J. (2013). *Digital disruption: Unleashing the next wave of
innovation*. Las Vegas, NV: Amazon Publishing.

This book explores how technology has led to great change from
disruptive innovation and how to shift your mind-set to be progressively more "disruptive" when looking to innovate. This is a discussion
of the changes taking place in all aspects of the market and the unfore-
seeable end to the accelerated pace of transformation.

Nussbaum, B. (2013). *Creative intelligence: Harnessing the power to create, connect, and inspire.* New York: HarperCollins Publishers.

This book is more focused on the individual exploration of creativity and how to develop, nurture, and cultivate it from yourself and others. It discusses the different types of creativity and how to develop and use creative ability to solve problems and create change in a world that is itself rapidly changing.

Index

About the Authors

Dr. Robert D. Hisrich is the Garvin Professor of Global Entrepreneurship and director of the Walker Center for Global Entrepreneurship at Thunderbird School of Global Management. He is also president of H&B Associates, a marketing and management-consulting firm he founded, and has been involved in the start-up of numerous global companies.

Professor Hisrich received his BA from DePauw University, his MBA, and PhD degrees from the University of Cincinnati, and honorary doctorate degrees from Chuvash State University (Russia) and the University of Miskolc (Hungary). Prior to joining Thunderbird, Dr. Hisrich was the A. Malachi Mixon III Chaired Professor of Entrepreneurial Studies at the Weatherhead School of Management, Case Western Reserve University. Dr. Hisrich was a Fulbright Professor at the International Management Center in Budapest, Hungary, in 1989. In 1990 and 1991, he was again named a Fulbright Professor in Budapest at the Foundation for Small Enterprise Economic Development, where he also held the Alexander Hamilton Chair in Entrepreneurship. Dr. Hisrich has held or now holds visiting professorships at the University of Ljubljana (Slovenia), the Technical University of Vienna (Austria), the University of Limerick (Ireland), Donau University (Austria), Queensland University of Technology (Australia), the University of Puerto Rico, and the Massachusetts Institute of Technology.

He has authored or coauthored 30 books, including *Entrepreneurship: Starting, Developing, and Managing a New Enterprise,* 9th edition (2013—translated into 13 languages), *Governpreneurship: Establishing a Thriving Entrepreneurial Spirit in Government* (2013), *Corporate Entrepreneurship* (2012), *International Entrepreneurship: Starting, Developing, and Managing a Global Venture,* 2nd edition (2012), *Technology Entrepreneurship: Value Creation, Protection, and Capture* (2010), *The 13 Biggest Mistakes That Derail Small Businesses and How to Avoid Them* (2004), and *The Woman Entrepreneur* (1986). Dr. Hisrich has written over 300 articles on entrepreneurship, international business management, and venture capital, which have appeared in such journals as *The Academy of Management Review*, *California Management Review*, *Columbia Journal of World Business*, *Journal of Business Venturing*, *Sloan Management Review*, and *Small Business Economics*. He has served on the editorial boards of the *Journal of Business Venturing*, *Entrepreneurship Theory and Practice*, *Journal of Small Business Management*, and *Journal of International Business and Entrepreneurship*. Besides designing and delivering management and entrepreneurship programs to U.S. and foreign businesses and governments, particularly in transition economies, Dr. Hisrich has instituted academic and training programs such as the university/industry training program in Hungary, a high school teachers entrepreneurship training program in Russia, and an Institute of International Entrepreneurship and Management in Russia. He has also been involved in starting and growing numerous ventures in the United States and other countries.

Dr. Claudine Kearney lectures and researches at University College Dublin, Quinn School of Business. She completed her postdoctoral fellowship at Thunderbird School of Global Management in Arizona in 2010. She holds a PhD and MBS from the University College Dublin, Michael Smurfit Graduate Business School. Dr. Kearney's research pursuits are focused on entrepreneurship and innovation with special interests in antecedents and outcomes of corporate entrepreneurship in private and public sector organizations; strategic entrepreneurship and innovation management in small and medium enterprises (SMEs) and large corporations, the emergence of entrepreneurship in SMEs. She is currently pursuing a number of joint international research projects within her specialism. Dr. Kearney has designed and delivered numerous entrepreneurship and management programs at undergraduate and postgraduate level. She has extensive experience lecturing undergraduate bachelor's degree programs and postgraduate MSc and MBA programs in the areas of entrepreneurship, innovation management, new venture start-up as well as strategic management and international business. She has lectured in seven countries across the United States, Europe, and Asia and recently held a visiting professorship in entrepreneurship and strategy at the University of Groningen, the Netherlands. Dr. Kearney serves on editorial boards and has published numerous academic journal articles, a book titled *Corporate Entrepreneurship: How to Create a Thriving Entrepreneurial Spirit in Your Company* (with Dr. Hisrich, 2011), book chapters, and conference papers.

⑤SAGE research**methods**

The essential online tool for researchers from the world's leading methods publisher

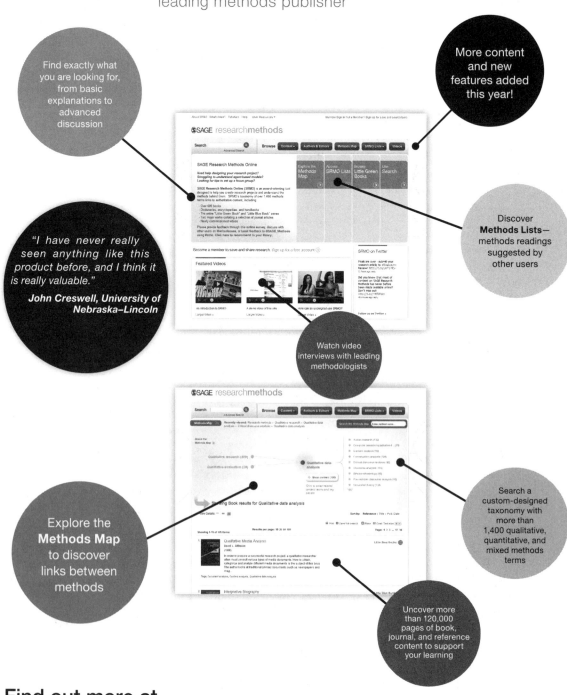

Find exactly what you are looking for, from basic explanations to advanced discussion

More content and new features added this year!

"I have never really seen anything like this product before, and I think it is really valuable."

John Creswell, University of Nebraska–Lincoln

Discover **Methods Lists**—methods readings suggested by other users

Watch video interviews with leading methodologists

Explore the **Methods Map** to discover links between methods

Search a custom-designed taxonomy with more than 1,400 qualitative, quantitative, and mixed methods terms

Uncover more than 120,000 pages of book, journal, and reference content to support your learning

Find out more at
www.sageresearchmethods.com